CWA1512209

THE TYNEHAM MANUSCRIPTS
ENIGMA

By John Randolf Scott

Copyright © 2015 John Randolf Scott

All rights reserved.

ISBN-10:1539329143

ISBN-13: 978-1539329145

DEDICATION

Jane Horton, Mary Tyler,
Doctor John Leiden and
the unknown man in the car park in
Tyneham

Copyright cover photo: present day remains of the Tyneham Rectory reproduced by permission of Shaun Matthews.

CONTENTS

PREFACE 7
INTRODUCTION 9
THE JOB 11
THE PROPOSITION 34
THE HOUSE..40
THE EARLY DOCTOR..53
THE YOUNG DOCTOR..62
THE FACTOR 70
THE BOAT 81
VENICE 89
THE BLACKSMITH...97
THE CARPENTER 109
CHRISTMAS 119
THE CLOCKMAKER 125
SAILING 130
A BROKEN LEG 136
SWIMMING 149
ROADS...154
OIL LAMPS 164
THE GREAT PLAGUE 176
THE FIRE OF LONDON..183
THE LATHE 192
THE STEAM PISTON 204
LONDON 218
THE PRIVY...227
TRAGEDY 234

PREFACE

On the 10th October of 2015 I was with my son and his wife and family visiting the south coast of England and we happened to be close to the village of Tyneham, which I knew had been requisitioned by the War Office in 1943 during World War II for servicemen training for the coming Normandy landings. The entire village was vacated and it has remained that way since. The village is a living window on the past. It is currently a gunnery range and only accessible at certain times.

After looking at the crumbling ruins and a quick walk around the museum I returned to my car where I was approached by an elderly man. He told me that as a very young boy, he and an older boy entered the dangerous forbidden area in the summer of 1950 and broke into the old Rectory, where he found some papers wrapped in rags in a hole in the wall. He took the papers to read at home, but could not understand the writing so he hid the papers because he didn't want to be caught for stealing. He felt guilty all his life about this episode, so he asked me, as a complete stranger, to return the papers to the rightful owners on his behalf.

Before I returned the papers into the care of the Army I read and photographed the series of memoirs in order to write this book.

I am no scholar of Elizabethan or 17th century English but I believe my understanding of the text is reasonably accurate despite the dialect words, the poor grammar and spelling, no paragraphs and no punctuation apart from full stops, and surprisingly no corrections. The whole manuscript is continuous, separated only by dates. The style is terse and descriptive rather than literary. I took the liberty of adding chapters and punctuation to the transcripts for greater clarity.

It is important to bear in mind that the young girl who wrote these accounts was poorly educated with a restricted vocabulary who lived in a small rural community so she would have been unfamiliar with 'modern English' of the times and unaware of national events outside her immediate environment. This is very much a parochial view of the times, except for the arrival of the foreigner, Doctor John Leiden.

INTRODUCTION

For those of you who are not familiar with 17th century English history, this brief synopsis will help to put you in the picture so that you can better appreciate this personal account of the times written by the young housemaid.

The century began with King James I on the throne (1603). He was also King James VI of Scotland. Although the crowns were united, the countries only became the United Kingdom in 1704. Amongst his legacy is the renowned King James translation of the Bible into English of the time. He died in 1625 and was succeeded by Charles I who was intent on demonstrating that he, the King, ruled the country and not the 'democratic' Parliament. The King's supporters (Cavaliers) went to war with the Parliamentarians (Roundheads), which raged between 1642 and 1649 and was eventually won by the Parliamentarians, resulting in the execution of the King in 1649. A short civil war broke out again between supporters of Charles II, but again the Parliamentarians won in 1651, and a Commonwealth was established under the leadership of Oliver Cromwell, the self styled Protector. Charles II was restored to the throne in 1660, but was later deposed and replaced by William of Orange in 1688 who brought with him peace between the English and the Dutch.

These were turbulent, violent times. Regardless of who was King, the ruling establishment were intent on keeping the rich, rich and the poor, poor. The rigid class system inhibited the opportunities to bridge the divide, although wealth helped. A wealthy merchant class was developing, and London was becoming the leading economic centre of Europe, gradually replacing the Dutch economic giants of the day. Trade was booming and the New World (America) was developing fast. England had a powerful Navy to support trade and to protect the nation.

The events described in the Tyneham manuscripts took place in the seven years between 1662 and 1669. In this time London experienced the Great Plague of 1665 followed by the Great Fire which destroyed virtually the whole of the inner city.

CHAPTER 1

The job

Munday 14 April 1662

Here be my letters writ in my own hand by me, Jane Horton.

The letters be my goodest but the paper be ruffe and poore.

ABCDEFGHIJKLM

OPQRSTUVWXYZN

abcdefghijklm

nopqrstuvwxyz

1 2 3 4 5 6 7 8 9 10 11 12

(Jan Leiden C.L.)

Munday 14 April 1662

Herein payper tis writ by me as the master sayeth my letters be dayntie, and he giveth me a quille with a brass poynte and much gray payper to wryte apon, which I doth cover in wax linen lest strayngers doth read my words .

I be Jane Horton of 8 and 10 years, daughter of Thomas Horton, saddle mayker, in the beste companie of Mary of lyke age, daughter of James Tyler, sayle mayker, alle of Wareham. We doth creepe away in secrette from prayer one Sunday in the month of March in the year of our Lord 1661 to seeke faire werke at the neuwe house in Tyneham for goodlie reward now that werke in the fields be done. Nowte else behold for pottage, save the bawdie house which be a vyle outrayge and Mary be of the sayme mynde. The pathe to Tyneham be trodde by man and beaste and be much brokke and maketh sore our feete.

We doth present to the master of the house who speaketh moste straynge for he be forayne. Withe modest countaynance we pleadeth his pleasure for service, and after diverse inquyrie he doth grante us werke withe a covenante for us to maketh our marke. Methinks the covenante be forayne ways. Mary be not goode withe words so I readeth the payper in awe for we must hath consent of Sire by 7 days. Me and Mary be moste joyous for we hath work withe fynne reward and such kyndness by that gentleman.

My Sire be moste willinge to mayketh a marke for he be payed a silver shillinge by the weeke and I be payed a shillinge by the day. I must pray on Sundays and visite my familie on the Saturday and Mary the sayme.

The gentleman be a leecher which oft be called phisker and must knoweth our infirms but I hast not ills and no concernes.

On the firste day the gentleman doth tayke our paypers and mayketh his marke as John Lyden, doctor of medicine in Hollande. Then he asketh yette more apon infirms and menses (and) commandeth (us) to weare a belt withe cleane wool pads on days of bleedinge which must be putte to fyre. He telleth us that tutors in readinge, writinge and numbers wilt come and Mistress Price of Steeple wilt tutor us in womens werke.

Violente ways be forbidden for alle at punishmente, else endinge be unto goode reason by both at other tymes.

Thence we doth passe in the Great Hall which be moste large to the stayrs and atop the lavatorium with tyles arounde. Without ado the master taketh our petticotes tille we be nayked and I be frit at what beholds but Mary showeth no concernes. The master doth look very close to our teeth and bodies and woman parts and doth combe our haire, which maketh me blushe. In a quicke momente the master sayeth that we be with vermin and then he doth disrobe tille nayked and doth powder us and giveth us French soappe (and) asketh our consentes to cutte the haire of our bodies. Mary sayeth yea whilst I was shy but giveth my nodde. The master then taketh a fynne blayde and cutte away our haire with grayte tenderness. Thence to the pluvia that maketh warme rayne. He doth wash and dry us with blankettes verie complete. This feeleth moste straynge for I feel more cleene than ever before. The master doth commande that we baythe in this manner by the day lest the vermin doth come agayne and to brush our teeth withe creeme twice by day for sweetness of breth. The master mayketh the creem withe birch sap, spirits, fynne chalk powder and mint from the garden.

In the bedchamber which be huge, a shift and under petticote and blue top petticote and a black bodice of woole and linen stockinges awayte and soft feete covers which be called makasins.

Them be so neuwe and quaynt. Mary doth twerle and shew her layce tryms. The master then giveth us combes and brushes. My frit be worth nowte, the master is a gentleman.

Now he sheweth to us the privy and in what manner to cleane our buttocks with woole wypers and what manner to wash the blue and whyte basin to wayste,

14

and what manner to wynde the clocke, and sette the calendar in the pharma.

The kitchen is wonderous large withe divers cupbords arounde and wyte marble for cuttinge foods. There be water in pypes and a wash tubbe of stone. In mornings we must fill the butte in the roof with a pump by hand. The pantrie be so fulle there be nowte room spare. The master commandeth that we do tayke food equal together thrice by day. There be a yron fyre and oven in the corner, asyde be a cupborde to dry clothes. Candles be chaynged by day and soute be wyped cleene.

Lether bootes be worne in the garden which hath chickens for eggs, cows for milke, pigs and a horse which we must cleene and feed by the day. The garden be sown withe divers vegtaybles and mennie herbes for phisics. Never before hast been my plezure to share such a fynne house and goodest livinge. Prayse be unto the goode Lord for alle his mercies.

Munday 14 April 1662

This is the first memoir following the alphabet exercises. It was written shortly after Jane Horton and

Mary Tyler started working as housemaids to Doctor Leiden at his new house in Tyneham. Both girls were poorly educated, which we can deduce from the lack of punctuation and paragraphs, and the strange spelling, although to be fair to Jane there were no dictionaries at that time. Probably neither had ever been to school, but their mothers had probably taught them to read and write and count with numbers at a very basic level. The doctor arranged for tutors to privately teach the girls. Mrs Price, a dressmaker from Steeple, came once a week to teach the girls her skills. The doctor also lectured them in history, geography and philosophy on an informal basis. Jane was the more proficient writer, which is probably why the doctor encouraged her to keep a diary, rather than Mary. Perhaps the doctor himself intended reading the diary, which might explain the alphabet exercise at the beginning to help decipher the writing.

The alphabet exercise is the only document that bears the signature of John Leiden, although he spelt it Jon or possibly Jan or even Ian. Despite this example signature, Jane managed to spell it incorrectly as John Lyden. Following this signature there are two letters C and L. These letters most likely stand for *'cum laude'* – the Latin for 'with honours', as if he was acting as a tutor and grading Jane's written work. It is a measure of her unfamiliarity with written documents that she elected to write across the page instead of down the page.

It is worth noting here that in the mid 17th century, good quality white writing paper was extremely expensive in England, which accounts for the fact that Jane was using poor quality grey paper, possibly even left over scrap paper from the doctor's student days in Leiden. High quality paper making had not yet been established in 17th century England and was still a closely guarded secret in Spain and Italy.

On average the grey paper weight is 100 gsm and varies between 60 gsm and 150 gsm but it is many times thicker and less dense than ordinary writing paper. The creamy yellowing of aged paper is entirely masked by the heavy grey coloration. The fact that these non acidic manuscripts have not been exposed to light or the atmosphere for 350 years probably accounts for the apparent lack of the usual signs of ageing. Certainly the newspaper used to wrap the manuscripts since 1950 exhibits heavy yellowing in just 65 years, but this is probably due to the acidic nature of newsprint in the 1950s. We don't know how the manuscripts were stored between 1950 and the present day, possibly in a biscuit tin beneath a pile of childhood mementoes including a newspaper, at the back of a cupboard or on top of a wardrobe, but we do know that they were wrapped in waxed linen for the previous 300 years because Jane tells us so.

This poor quality paper was probably re-cycled book paper from a printer and as such would contain no fillers such as chalk or clay and little or no gelatine or alum to prevent ink from bleeding. It was little better than what we would describe as 'blotting' paper; straight from the deckle and mould with no pressing or calendering. This re-worked paper would have been non acidic paper and less prone to yellowing with age. The re-work pulping process was so poor that periodically letters of the previous text can be found embedded in the paper and even these fragments show no yellowing.

Yet Jane manages to write very clearly on the rough uneven surface, although she did complain and obviously had some difficulty judging the quantity of ink on the quille. In this respect Jane obviously has a natural talent for calligraphy. Whilst her spelling and vocabulary are under developed, her handwriting is exceptionally clear and precise. At some time in her childhood somebody must have spent a great deal of time training her to write this well.

Normally the ink used at that time would have been iron gall which in itself is acidic, but Dr Leiden preferred his own ink that he made from lampblack and gum Arabic. Iron gall ink would have been useless on the paper that Jane was using. Due to the very small particle size of lampblack, this ink probably flowed more smoothly particularly when used as drawing ink, and was not prone to bleeding, although we know that the doctor also used graphite pencils. Candles and lamps around the house would have been a ready source of lampblack. Indeed, we know that one of the servant's duties was to clean the 'smoke dishes' above candles and lamps every day. The purpose of the smoke dishes was to clean the soot from the flame rather than let the black soot drift around the house or accumulate on the walls and ceilings. These 'dishes' were probably small shallow ceramic bowls that might have contained aromatic fluids to perfume the air.

Jane also tells us that she is writing with a quill that has a brass point. She doesn't say whether the brass point (knib) is an invention of the doctor or whether such points were common at the time. It is unreasonable to expect Jane to explain everything about her world. She does her best to make a note of those things that she finds unusual or strange, probably because the doctor's house was full of novelties.

Jane's account reflects her more introverted and measured personality, but we have no idea how Mary felt other than small observations by Jane, although in later memoirs we discover that Mary is much more outspoken and outgoing.

Both girls were attractive, impressionable eighteen year olds who had taken the bold and enterprising decision to sneak away after church one Sunday and make the arduous journey on foot from their homes in

Wareham, to Tyneham (5 miles) in order to seek a job as servant girls, in the innocent, naive hope that it would be the first step out of the pit of grinding poverty. Spring planting in the fields was over and there was no prospect of any wages until harvest time, even for soup, except by earning money in a bawdy house which she considered to be a 'vile outrage'.

At this point it would be appropriate to review exactly what being a household servant entailed, at that time. Servants were basically slaves with a paltry salary. Servants usually 'lived in'; they lived in the same house as their employer. Servant's quarters were often poorly furnished, cold and completely separate from the part of the premises occupied by the employer and his family. Some premises even had separate staircases exclusively for the use of servants to keep them away from the employer and his family. Servants were merely goods and chattels to be used and abused, just as slaves had been similarly used for centuries. Servants were often beaten for making mistakes. Female servants were particularly at risk because like slaves, their employer owned them body and soul, particularly body. It was a widely held belief amongst employers that they had a right to expect sexual favours from their female servants. Even the famous diarist Samuel Pepys tried it on with his maid, Deb Willet, until his wife found out.

On the plus side, they were paid quarterly, even if it was a pittance. Employment was generally seven days a week from dawn till dusk with very little free time to themselves. If servants were lucky they joined the employer's family on visits. Sometimes employers would provide uniforms, but this was normally just for show. Servants were also provided with food, but this was often not the same as the luxurious meals that servants cooked and prepared for their masters.

Imagine the surprise and delight of the two girls when the doctor announced that he would employ them both as housemaids. To their further surprise they were presented with a written 'covenant', or what we would nowadays call a contract of employment. This set out the terms, their duties and the employer's obligations. Such contracts were unheard of in those days. Sadly we do not have a copy of the original document, although Jane's account gives us a broad overview.

Written agreements were extremely unusual in any context at that time, least of all regarding employment. Jane even comments that this was a foreign concept. A gentleman's word was his bond. Putting stuff in writing was an affront to a gentleman's honour because it implied that he might break his word.

The house was both huge and luxurious compared to the homes that the girls had come from (a later memoir describes the house in considerable detail). Jane is reluctant or ashamed to describe her former lowly lifestyle, and who can blame her. We can surmise that the homes that the girls had come from were probably rented two roomed cottages with reed-thatched roofs. If they were lucky the kitchen had a brick chimney, otherwise it would be an open fire with a hole in the roof. The other room would be the family bedroom where the whole family slept, probably on the floor on woollen blankets. Again, if they were lucky the floor would be paved with rough stone flags, otherwise it would be just dry trampled mud. Outside there may have been a wooden shack privy (toilet), but most likely they used a chamber pot which they would empty into the nearest stream, river or open drain. Water would be drawn daily from the nearest hand pump or stream. The whole family would eat from wooden bowls with their fingers. There was no bathroom. Clothes and bed linen would be washed, without soap, in the nearest river, probably once or twice a year. The family would have taken a bath at the same time in cold river water and still partially clothed. More than likely the windows in the home contained no glass: they were either open to the elements or had a small piece of oil soaked linen nailed to the frame to allow some light in and to keep out the wind and rain. On the whole it was a dirty, miserable existence that was just about bearable in summer but intolerable in winter.

The 'covenant' required that the girls submit to a medical examination to make sure they were fit and sound and carried no diseases. The girls had probably never been examined before and had no idea what to expect. Mary took this in her stride probably because the rewards far outweighed the temporary indignity. Jane was more apprehensive and clearly reluctant to expose her flesh to a stranger, even if he was a doctor. Despite her misgivings, Jane too could see the benefits and rewards, and finally conceded.

The medical examination was conducted in the tiled *lavatorium* (bathroom) at the top of the stairs to the upper floor, where the girls were stripped naked. The doctor examined them in thorough detail for signs of disease or malfunctions. He also examined their teeth and breasts and confirmed that they would be provided with toothbrushes and cream (made by the doctor) which they must use twice a day. The doctor obviously told them that they both had fleas and lice and immediately treated them with his Dalmatian dusting powder (pyrethrum insecticide). He also provided each girl with a personal hairbrush and a fine-toothed lice comb. The doctor set aside their old clothes to be burnt.

He asked each girl about their previous medical history and about their menstrual periods and how they dealt with the problem. In order to maintain their personal cleanliness, the doctor insisted that they must wear special pads on bleeding days. A fresh pad must be worn each day. The pad consisted of a linen sock attached to a belt with buttons and loops. Inside the sock was a raw woollen pad that must be removed and burnt after use. The sock had to be soaked in cold water to remove any blood, and then it had to be boiled and washed in water. Compared to the contemporary primitive alternatives, this arrangement was the pinnacle of personal hygiene for its time.

At this point the proceedings become a little bizarre. The doctor then asked each girl if she wanted her armpits and pubis shaved to remove body hair to make it easier to keep free of vermin (lice and fleas), a common practice at the time in the middle east. Mary volunteered without a second thought, whereas Jane only reluctantly conceded so as not to be left out. The doctor promptly produced a bar of French soap and a razor made from Damascus steel. The girls had experienced nothing like this before, but probably assumed that this was what high-class ladies normally endured.

Obviously the girls were unaccustomed to taking a bath. The dusting powder needed to be washed off and their heads needed checking that the powder had done its job. There was no conventional bath. Instead the doctor showed them the *'pluvia'* (Latin for rain), which was a tiled alcove with a hot water sprinkler above it, operated by two brass faucets. The doctor disrobed to demonstrate how the shower worked and set about showing them how to use soap and bathe themselves to clean their bodies thoroughly.

At first sight, all this might seem a little extreme by modern medical standards, but bear in mind that modern doctors expect their patients to know about personal hygiene, and that patients already know how to bath themselves. Nowadays we take a lot for granted. The contract probably also required that every year each girl would be medically examined, and if necessary treatment for any malady would be given free.

The girls were then shown their separate bedrooms where their uniforms were set out on each bed. The uniform consisted of a short white linen shift, a linen underskirt with a lace hem, a bright blue top skirt and a black woollen bodice. Fine white linen stockings that tied below the knee (elastic didn't exist) were also provided. There was no underwear because women at that time did not wear underwear. For nightwear they had a short linen shift. It was a house rule to wear soft leather indoor slippers that the doctor called 'makasins' (a native American word). Knee length leather boots were provided for outside wear.

The girls dressed and presented themselves for inspection in the Great Hall, where the doctor showed them the daily task of winding up the pendulum clock. The tutors would teach them how to tell the time (the clock only had one hand showing hours). They were also shown how to change candles, and wipe the soot dishes. Downstairs there was also another 'privy' just like the one upstairs. Another daily task was to burn the used woollen 'wipers' in the box beside the privy.

They also had the daily task of setting the date on the calendar in the 'pharma'. We know from a later memoir that the doctor commissioned a calendar to be made a by a clock-maker in London (William Parsons) when he purchased the pendulum clock while his house was being built.

Jane barely mentions this daily task so I think we can safely assume that it was a perpetual calendar with a gear train driving engraved barrels with the day number, month name and year number. A simple knob or lever would be used to index the day barrel, and the internal gears would index the months and years automatically. At that time England was still using the Julian Calendar where the year change occurs on 25th March (New Year's Day), and every fourth year was a leap year, hence the apparent discrepancy in the date sequence at the top of each memoir because January, February and March followed December. As a result, February 1662 would nowadays be counted as February 1663.

I suspect that Jane copied her dates directly from this calendar, which would account for her using numeric day numbers not ordinal numbers, and spelling the months correctly while the days of the week were spelt incorrectly. I believe this is a reasonable supposition in the light of no direct evidence from Jane.

The girls changed into boots and were taken to see the cowshed, pigpen and stable for the master's horse. Next to the cowshed there was a wooden chicken coup. The girls were required to milk the cows daily, collect the eggs and let the chickens out into the garden and to groom the horse.

The garden was planted with vegetables and medicinal herbs. There was no lawn. Outside the kitchen door there was a hand water pump that drew water from a cistern below. The cistern was fed from local spring water. Every morning the girls had to fill the main house water butt using a force pump. There is no mention of emptying chamber pots so we must assume the specially designed privy bowls could be flushed. Jane mentions that they were shown how to wash the privy bowl, but I suspect that this meant that they were shown how to open the flush faucet and for how long.

Preparing and cooking food was one of the duties listed in the contract, so the doctor showed them the kitchen. In the left hand corner there was a wood fired iron furnace with an oven on each side. Behind the grate there was a brick chimney and alongside the chimney there was a drying cabinet from floor to ceiling. In wet weather clothes could be dried in the warm air in the cabinet. Around the walls there were many cupboards containing cooking pots, glassware and crockery. In the opposite corner there was a pantry for storing food. Beneath the window (which had real glass) there was a glazed earthenware washing tub about a foot deep, with brass faucets above, that turned the hot and cold water on or off. There was not a single house in the village, including Tyneham House, that could boast hot and cold running water. Around the remaining floor space next to the walls there were wooden shelves with white Purbeck marble tops.

The two girls and the doctor would eat the same food at the same time together at table in the kitchen. At special times the table would be set in the Great Hall. After a meal the cooking pots and crockery must be cleaned and washed. Surplus food had to be set aside for the pigs. The contract stated that food would be taken three times daily. It was the employer's obligation to supply and pay for all food.

In terms of salary, the girls would be paid a silver shilling a day for seven days each week. There would be no work on Saturdays or Sundays, but the girls had to donate one day's pay to their parents and they must visit their parents once a week to make that donation. They must also attend church on Sunday morning.

By the standards of the time this salary was more than twice the going rate even allowing for the parental donation. The parents would have been overjoyed too, because the extra shilling a week would have made a significant increase to the family income.

The last part of the contract would have dealt with dismissal and punishment. Basically the employer could not summarily dismiss staff without good grounds, such as theft or gross disobedience or misconduct. The girls were free to resign at any time on notice of probably one month. Violence at any time by either party was forbidden, particularly as punishment.

Even by today's standards this is a very reasonable contract. It is a pity that this contract was 350 years before its time. Little wonder that the girls were so overjoyed. They had made a giant leap out of the poverty trap rather than just a small step. It was 'a dream come true'.

Throughout the document Jane refers to John Leiden more formally as the 'master' but I prefer doctor. Obviously she would become less formal with time, but in her memoirs she later refers to him by the initials M.J. which presumably stand for Master John. Perhaps she lacked the courage of addressing him by his first name in case it implied lack of respect. I will take the liberty of using his first name.

CHAPTER 2
The Proposition

Munday 28 April 1662

By the grace of our Lord lyfe be joyous and happy but I liveth under the shadow of giltte and must putte my head to payper to see cleare sense.

Mary doth flirte withe the master in the manner as a Jezabel. Her breasts nere falle from her bodice and she doth embrayce him on the lippes and twerle her petticotes to provoke his luste and doth talk much of amorous rytes. Methinks she hath given her maydenly trezure to the master alreadie, but it be without proofe.

At dinner the master asketh who wilt warm my bed tonytte and Mary wast so quicke to giveth her nodde, but the master doth stay his hand for me to ponder. I be all confusion twixt desire and dowtte. If I refuse then perchance my service be ended and I hasth not fayvore with the master as Mary. If I doth consente what doth befalle if I am with chylde then it be the sayme bothe ways for I be loste so I doth consent to the plezure of the master to keepeth his equal fayvore twixt Mary and me. The warmynge word doth now bringe grayte merriment twixt alle.

I be frit and shy in the bedchaymber but the master be moste gentle and tender with soft hands and close embrayces until his vigors maketh me luz all sense and tremble. On the morrow I doth awayke with new passyons in my hearte and in awe of my feelinges of the nytte. I be a fulle woman and prowde but my head doth naggge with giltte. Methinks my consent be sinfulle for we be not marryed.

I ponder. The Law be clear that a man doth have but one wyfe but hath no words for his number of mistresses. By consent (I) brayketh no Law therebye nor canst I be sinfulle. My head be cleare of giltte this instante and I canst enjoy these plezures. Mary be not alone in her passyon for the master.

Prayse be unto the Lord for the passyon in my hearte

Munday 28 April 1662

Picture the situation: two impressionable teenage girls secure a plum, well-paid job with a handsome, talented, wealthy gentleman as the boss. It is a 'live in' job in which they spend most of their time in the company of the boss. The boss is charismatic, charming and treats the girls with consideration and respect, unlike other men of the period. Phrased in this way, it is obviously a recipe for a deeper 'relationship' to develop between them. At the very least we could expect the girls to have a crush on the boss. The role and position of women at the time was that they had the status of chattels. Inbred subservience and obedience would have left the girls extremely vulnerable.

The doctor, on the other hand, lived in an age of total male dominance with few rules and regulations to govern his thoughts and deeds. For example, the age of consent was only thirteen. Rape was often exceedingly difficult to prove (as now) and in many areas it was common to pay off the victim. In Wales, compensation was a legal option as punishment for rape. Legal sex (marriage) was limited to one wife but did not require her consent. Rape within marriage did not exist: a view that persisted for centuries. Sex outside marriage had no restrictions other than mild social disapproval. It was clearly a man's world.

The next memoir from Jane was written about two weeks after her first account. We could take this as an indication of the importance that she attaches to the events she describes.

Jane begins with some observations concerning Mary's brazen flirtation with John. She adjusted the neckline of her shift and bodice to expose more of her breasts. She often returned a peck on the cheeks by John with a kiss on the lips. She skipped and danced, twirling her skirts to reveal her legs, making sure John was watching. Mary also had a habit of raising 'amorous rites' (sex) as a discussion topic over dinner. Jane has no proof that Mary and John are having sex but she has her suspicions, or perhaps she is jealous and feels that she is being left behind and missing out, but doesn't yet have the courage to bring the subject into the open.

Her turmoil is resolved when John does the job for her by casually asking 'Who will warm my bed tonight?'. Mary immediately volunteers, but John insists that Jane should also have her say. This really puts Jane on the spot. She was already a victim of indoctrination since birth by the unjust, unfair and corrupt society of the time. She was possibly in love with John already, (who can say?), but she felt guilty and possibly ashamed of her desires and feelings. To complicate matters further she was under pressure from the knowledge that her employment might be at risk and that this would affect her parent's income too. What did she do? She did what all humans do when faced with a dilemma: she rationalised her moral misgivings in order to square her conscience. She made her own decision in a way that she could live with.

Jane obviously enjoyed her night of love making but felt guilty the following day. However, she argued in her mind that she had broken no laws, therefore she had not been sinful. If a married man had sex outside marriage then that was sinful but if he was unmarried and had sex with a mistress then that only carried mild social disapproval but wasn't regarded as sin. It was not unusual for common people to assume that the law of the land was the same as the law of the bible, i.e. breaking the law was not only criminal, but sinful too.

Whatever you may think of John, or Mary, you have to admire and respect Jane for working out how to beat her conscience. From that point on the word 'warming' was used as a familiar euphemism for sex.

CHAPTER 3
The House

Friday 9 May 1662

The house of the master be next the church of St Maryin Tyneham and be 6 rods at the front and fore (4) rods deepe with stone corners and walls of pumyce betwixt, with a chimnie at each end. Springe water cometh from Egliston in stone pypes to a bricke cellar in the garden nere to the kitchen. Fowle water be took to a bricke cellar at the end of the garden. The house be not grande lyke Tyneham House in the woodes but insyde it be a palace with no ryval.

The entrance door be thicke woode and stronge withe black yron hinges and bowltes. Insyde a porche withe a woode screen and a small door with a green window. Beyonde be the halle and wayters bench. By left the Pharma and by ryte the Grayte Halle with two glasse windows with hinges atop which stoppeth the rayne to falle insyde. The privie, and clocke and kitchen to the left and opposite be a whyte marble fyreplace and asyde the stayres.

The kitchen hath a stone wash tub beneath the window with pypes of hot and cold water. The yron fyre box hath ovens for breade and meats and a hot gritte box for the cloth presse withe 3 corners on the shelffe, which I never didst see before.

The master be moste firm that Mary and me always be welle presented and we must press his linen shirt by day and the blue kercheefe and the black breeches and brush his fynne woole doublette. On a Sunday he doth ware gray breeches and a red kercheefe and in rayne a black hatte.

The pantrie be fulle withe foode and nowte room for more. There be divers pots and glasse wares and drinkinge cuppes and china bowles and yron knives and spoones aplentie. In the midst a woode tayble and 4 chayres of good forme and all around whyte marble taybles and shelfes below. Tis hard werke by mornings to fille the water butte in the roofe by hand pumpe.

Atop stayrs be the lavatorium and privie next the bedchaymber of the master which hath a wyde soft bed and dressinge cupbordes and 2 windows and a small

41

clocke. Opposyte be my bedchaymber next the bedchaymber of Mary. My room hath a window and a smalle bed with a canvas bagge of dry beans and a top bagge of fethers with whyte linen sheets and blankettes of woolle. The bed hath no ryval for comforte and I doth sleppe most sownde. My room hath a dressinge room and drawers for private matters. Mary hath the sayme with no favore twixt us.

Candlestycks be beyonde the countinge but cleaninge wax be moste tyrsome but soute dishes for inke be simple' We canst not complayn in such a palace. The Lord hath so blessed us with goodest fortune.

Friday 9 May 1662

This particular memoir was written about a month after Jane and her companion Mary moved into the house built by Doctor John Leiden next to St Mary's church in Tyneham. It is a reasonably detailed description of the house and its more unusual features that make it stand out from houses of the same type in the mid 17th century.

Currently there is a 19th century Rectory standing on the site where John Leiden's house was originally built.

She describes the house as being next to St Mary's church but this unlikely because there is a graveyard next to the church. The current Rectory is next to the graveyard and John Leiden's house would have occupied the same site. From Jane's description it appears to bear a remarkable similarity to much of the later rectory, which suggests that the present rectory was essentially a re-build or modification of the original building with an extension added to the rear of the premises.

Access to the site is by a pathway around the back of the church and graveyard, although a footpath also exists that passes by the 'ponds', past the cottages, the church and the school. Apart from horses and carts, normal visitors on foot would have used the short cut path

The remains of the current Rectory include several stone built outbuildings but when Dr Leiden built the original house these outbuildings were probably wooden structures to house the pig pens, the cowshed and the stable for the horse.

It is unlikely that Jane was interested in, or even knew about the terms and how the doctor acquired the land to build his house. In all probability the land was in the glebe of the rectory and would have been subject to annual tithes (10% land tax). The tithe was calculated on the value of agricultural products and a valuation of any buildings. In this case it would have been a small nominal sum. We also don't know who built the house, but most likely it would have been a local builder in Wareham perhaps.

We only know, by calculating backwards, that the doctor must have started building in late 1660 after he returned from Venice, and it must have been finished before the girls arrived in April 1662. In between these two dates John was probably training to sail his kattumaram with frequent trips to and from London, delivering items like the pendulum clock, the calendar, the Delft toilet bowls, brass pipes and the pumice insulation, and generally keeping an eye on progress. Whilst the doctor could sail his craft alone, it is uncharacteristic of him to take such risks. It is most likely that he hired a fisherman with sea experience from Worbarrow to accompany him.

At the same time he was busy promoting and expanding his insecticide business, which must have become very successful because we learn from a later memoir that he gave the girls lavish presents.

We know nothing about the foundations of the house because there is no mention in Jane's account, except for a reference to the fact that the local spring by the path to Egliston was partially diverted (probably salt glazed earthenware pipes) to a brick built well close to the back entrance. There was probably an overflow pipe back to the original stream which emptied into the 'ponds' close to the row of buildings known as Rectory Cottages. A manual pump stood on top of the well. This was the only supply of drinking water to the house. Similarly, she mentions that waste water was carried in a pipe to a brick built underground cellar (septic tank) at the end of the garden.

The four corners of the building were built from blocks of Purbeck limestone, which can still be seen in what remains of the current rectory. The walls between the corners were probably made of limestone rubble rendered with mortar. We don't know for sure because Jane doesn't tell us, but we do know the building measured 6 rods by 4 rods (one rod equals five and a half feet). What we also know is that Dr Leiden procured a large quantity of pumice from a wine importer in London, who was using sacks of pumice, from Mount Teide in Tenerife, as packing to stabilise cargoes of Malmsey wine aboard ships. This pumice was used as insulation on the inside of all the external walls in the house. We don't know if it was mixed with lime mortar and plastered on, or whether it was inserted behind wood panelling, but I suspect the latter.

You might ask why the polymath doctor should go to such lengths to employ unusual, but very cheap, building materials to insulate his house at a time when insulation was unheard of, except in industries like iron smelting and glass making? At the beginning of the 17th century the government recognised that heavy industry and the Navy were depleting the forests of England so in 1609 the use of wood as an industrial fuel was banned and coal had to be used instead. It could have been in John's mind that this ban might be extended to the burning of wood in general. Insulation, and subsequent fuel economy would therefore make sense.

Inside the house on the side walls at each end there were two brick chimneys. One chimney served the big hearth in the Great Hall and the other served the furnace in the kitchen. In a later memoir we learn that they also used baskets of hot stones (night storage heaters) for additional heating. It is more than likely that when the new rectory was built, the original building was gutted, including the panelling and insulating material. Many additional fireplaces and two new chimneys were then needed to adequately heat the new uninsulated building.

Jane's account gives us a walk through view of the internal layout. She tells us that the front door was very heavy wood (probably re-worked oak from ships timbers) supported on iron gudgeon and pintle hinges. Inside there was a porch and a wooden partition with a central lighter door and a forest glass window (poor quality semi-obscure glass). Beyond the partition there was a small entrance hall with a bench immediately opposite (for waiting patients). To the left was a door to the *'pharma'*, (what we would call the doctor's surgery). To the right was a door leading to the Great Hall. The current remains of the rectory indicate that partition walls were erected to make the great hall into three smaller rooms, probably to make it easier heat in winter. Opposite this door inside the Great Hall was an impressive Purbeck marble fireplace. To the left of the fireplace was a stairway to the floor above (the stair well can still be seen in the remains of the rectory). Opposite the fireplace next to the entrance door was a privy and next to that was a door to the kitchen. In between the two doors stood the pendulum clock. At the bottom of the stairs there was a window, and along the front of the house there were two more windows. Unusually, the casement windows had hinges at the top, which nowadays would be called awning windows. Jane explains that when it rained, these windows did not allow the rain to fall inside the house.

The door from the Great Hall opened into the kitchen. In the opposite left hand corner there was a wood fired iron grate with an oven on each side, big enough to bake bread and roast meat. A grit box was always kept hot on the furnace for pressing clothes. The hot press (iron) was kept on a nearby shelf. The press consisted of a small triangular plate of brass with raised sides, probably about three inches deep and a hinged lid with a wood handle. Hot pea-sized gravel could be shovelled into the box and then the lid was snapped shut (similar devices are still used to this day in some parts of the world such as India). It is very likely that it was a condition of employment that the girls should press their garments whenever they intended to be seen in public.

The doctor liked his clothes to be pressed as well, in particular his linen shirt, breeches and his kerchief. According to Jane, the doctor normally wore a white linen shirt and a blue neck tie (scarf), with black trousers and jacket. Like womenfolk, men did not wear underwear at that time. In fact his linen shirt was considered as underwear so not much of it was on show to the public. On Sundays he would often wear grey linen trousers with a red neck tie, and if it was raining he wore a black hat. He probably looked smart and sober but certainly not flamboyant. What would have made the doctor stand out in a crowd was that he was clean shaven, and wore clean clothes that looked as good as new without creases, and he wore his sword on his back not at his side.

Beside the furnace there was a drying cabinet from floor to ceiling for drying clothes and bed linens. There was a window in the far wall and another window opposite the drying cabinet. Underneath this window there was a shallow wash-tub (sink) with hot and cold faucets. Next to the sink was the rear door to the garden and the manual water pump. Around the remaining space there were many shelves with thick Purbeck marble tops. On the walls there were several cupboards containing cooking pots, glassware and crockery. In the opposite corner there was a pantry for storing food. In the centre of the kitchen there was a stout wooden table and four chairs.

At the top of the stairs there was a window to one side, and a door to the '*lavatorium*' (a combined toilet and bathroom). This room was tiled (floor and walls) with blue and white Delft tiles. The toilet bowl and washbasin were also Delft china. The '*pluvia*' (shower) was supplied with hot and cold water from wooden water butts in the roof space above. Jane mentions that the first task of the day was to fill these butts with water using the hand pump in the kitchen. The pipes and fittings were made of brass. There was one window overlooking the rear garden. Another door in the *lavatorium* gave access to the doctor's bedchamber.

The stairway also gave access to a corridor or landing to the front of the house, with two doors on the left, leading to two bedrooms occupied by the housemaids. In both of these bedrooms there were dressing rooms (wardrobes) that stretched along the walls next to the entrance doors. The room at the back had a window overlooking the rear garden (occupied by Mary) and the other had a window overlooking the front of the house (occupied by Jane). Both rooms had beds with a canvas mattress filled with dried beans covered by a canvas mattress stuffed with feathers. The beds had linen sheets and woollen blankets with feather filled cushions. Beside each bed there was a wooden chest with drawers, and a candlestick on top. Later, the windows were covered with muslin curtains and blue drapes.

Another door on the right from the corridor gave access to the master bedroom, which had a double bed with the same type of mattresses, sheets, blankets and cushions. The room had a window overlooking the front of the house and one window on the side of the house. There was a large dressing room (wardrobe) on one wall and two bedside chests with drawers and candlesticks. Again curtains and drapes were added later.

CHAPTER 4
The early doctor

Tewsday 27 May 1662

Oft tymes MJ taketh me and Mary to his bed for tayles of history or forayne landes which he telleth better than bookes. One tyme he telleth of his infante days in Scotlande and saylinge to the Neuwe Worlde withe a talle Sire with bearde and Madam fulle withe tears who he doth bare remember and himself amidst sickness, frit and vexed, before a storm maketh the shippe a wreck and alle aborde do leepe or perishe and the yunge master afloat withe a woode. In tyme he be washed ashore and wast took prisoner by naytives. The cheefe of the trybe taketh kynde of his plyte and rayseth the chylde as one of them. 8 summers passeth afore a Spanish shippe doth come for water and woode and come apon MJ with hunters and mayketh a rescue and doth slorter others. A priest of Portugal aborde the shippe sayeth the trybe be called Cherowkie and doth care for MJ and tutor his tunge and the Latin. In some days the shippe doth cometh apon a halfe dead saylor who be Jan Martens, a Dutchman, an enemie who be mayde prisoner in yrons. MJ hath sorrow for the prisoner and stealeth foode to ayde him. Nere to Cadiz the shippe be strucke by a moste violente storm which doth wreck the shippe on rocks. MJ doth fynde keys on a dead souldyer to free the Dutchman from chayns. In gratitude Jan Martens doth steale trezure for both and aydeth MJ to swimme. In Portugal them mayketh a brybe to a blacksmithe to stryke away the yrons and the both walketh 3 months to Hollande. Jan be in much hayste and doth rent his haire and beard in anger, and stealeth a fish boat to Lehaver which doth take fulle 20 days and thence do barter passage withe gold on a sweete smellinge shippe to Amsterdam which droppeth anker on 25 September in the Year of our Lord 1654. MJ hence doth call this day to be his birth and he be olde by 5 and 10 years, which he doth enjoye with the Dutchman for the firste tyme in wynne which mayketh his head to swimme. The Lord be praysed for the lyfe of our dear master.

Tewsday 27 May 1662

We know that the good doctor tutored the girls from time to time in history and geography, but these were not boring, structured lessons. Instead they were more like anecdotes from his personal experiences. The girls obviously adored these dramatic tales and were eager for more. In an age when entertainment was virtually non-existent, apart from the theatres in London, the dramas told by John carried more impact than TV does for us today. His frequent trips to London were the only source of news and gossip from the big city. For the girls this was like a personal TV news channel. In their turn the girls would pass on the news to the rest of the village, which no doubt elevated the status of the two girls.

It seems that John was born in Scotland, which at that time was a separate nation, not yet in union with England. At a very young age (probably four or five years old) he and his parents sailed to the New World (America) to start a fresh life. John probably didn't know why his parents undertook such a risky adventure, but he did have memories of being very seasick and miserable. Likewise he had no perception of how long the journey took. He only had memories of being cold, dirty and hungry, and memories of his mother weeping all the time. He only had fleeting memories of his father as being tall and bearded.

They had almost reached their destination when the ship was struck by a fearsome storm that blew them south and eventually wrecked the ship. As far as John could remember everybody was screaming and shouting as the ship fell apart. His parents lashed the child to a fallen timber to save him from drowning, and the next he remembers is waking up on a beach surrounded by native Indians. He was taken back to their camp still tied to the piece of timber. John believed the tribe were Cherokee Indians although they never referred to themselves by that name. The chief, for some inexplicable reason, adopted the shipwrecked boy into the tribe, where he spent the next eight summers (years) living as an Indian, speaking their tongue and learning their ways and culture.

He was out hunting one day with a small group from the tribe when they were confronted by a band of Spanish soldiers, whose ship had anchored off shore. The captain sent a party ashore to look for fresh water and timber to repair the ship. It was immediately apparent to the Spaniards that the young doctor was not a native and assumed he was a captive, so they 'rescued' him and slaughtered the rest of the hunting party.

A kindly priest on board the Spanish ship took the young lad under his wing and taught him Latin so that they could converse, as well as a few words of Spanish and Portuguese, because the priest was in fact Portuguese himself. It was this priest who told him that the savages were Cherokee because the ship was off the coast that they inhabited. Some time later the ship came upon a lone man on a raft, who it appears was the survivor of a wrecked Dutch merchantman. At the time, the Dutch were at war with Spain so the 'enemy' was immediately imprisoned and shackled in leg irons, regardless of the fact that the survivor was already half dead.

The Dutchman, Jan Martens by name, had a few words of English and was able to communicate with the young doctor at a very simple level, because John only had the vocabulary of a five year old. They were both unwitting guests aboard the ship, and perhaps this is why a bond developed between them. Soon the young lad was stealing food to keep the prisoner alive.

After about two and a half months the ship eventually arrived off Cadiz (on the coast of Spain), but was immediately hit by a violent storm from the south and was driven north and ran ashore on the rocks. Like everybody else, the soldier on guard scrambled to get off the ship to save himself, but he was struck by falling timbers, leaving the Dutchman locked up in chains. The young boy managed to find the keys on the dead soldier and released the Dutchman still in leg irons. Instead of escaping, the crafty Dutchman insisted that they should open the treasure vault because they had the soldier's keys. The Dutchman grabbed a leather bag of treasure just before the ship fell apart and pitched them into the sea.

Shipwrecks were not uncommon in those days, but surviving two wrecks in such a short time span was tempting providence and made a lasting impression on the young lad. The pair floated for some days clutching a large piece of ships timber and were finally washed ashore. To their surprise they discovered that they were in Portugal not Spain. The young lad made this discovery when he went looking for a blacksmith in the first town they encountered. The Dutchman bribed the blacksmith with a gold coin to strike off his leg irons, and then the pair set off to walk to Holland.

After about three months Jan got tired of walking and decided to hasten the journey by taking to the sea again, in a stolen fishing boat. It appears that Jan was a good seaman and kept to the French coast so that they could take on food and water more easily. Three weeks later they eventually arrived at the large Normandy port of Le Havre, where they purchased a passage on a home bound East India merchantman heading for Amsterdam, using gold coins from the treasure bag. John remembered very clearly the strong aromatic smell from the cargo aboard this ship.

John was about fifteen years old by the time the ship docked in Amsterdam on 25th September 1654. By this time John was conversing freely in Dutch. To mark his arrival, the young lad decided that this day would be his birthday and that he was 15 years old. To celebrate, Jan visited a goldsmith and changed some of the gold coins into usable Dutch coinage, which he divided equally, so that they could celebrate in style.

For the first time in his life the young doctor tasted wine and became mildly intoxicated. He was very happy to be back on dry land again.

This is as far as this account takes us. To summarise, we have John as a teenager who doesn't really know where or when he was born, but has adopted a false age and birthday, and an assumed birthplace and nationality. In addition he has acquired fluency in Dutch and has a working knowledge of Latin, Spanish, Portuguese and English, as well as fluency in an unspecified native Indian language. We only have the assumption of the priest that his tribe were Cherokee, but the priest never set foot on land and never met the tribe. Moreover, the priest only had the word of the ship's navigator of their current whereabouts. Their location was educated guesswork because navigation at that time in uncharted territory could have been wildly inaccurate. It is unlikely that the Spanish authorities were ever in pursuit of the pair because they only stole a small bag of treasure, which the salvage crew would have put down to 'lost at sea'.

What we can say with some certainty is that the young lad had learnt that people in chains or in prison are not necessarily bad people. He also learnt that the only way to travel long distances was by sea, and that ships are no match for the sea and can easily sink.

CHAPTER 5
The young doctor

Wenesday 18 June 1662

Me and Mary oft tymmes inquyre of MJ whyfore he doth come to passe in Tyneham and he telleth this tayle. In respect for his frienship with Jan Martens he tayketh his advyce to become a doctor at the Universitie in Leiden, but firste he must studie at school the Latin because all bookes of medecine be in that tunge. In that time he be a geste withe the familie of the Dutchman at the house of his cuson of the sayme age for they hath spare room. MJ be of goode memorie for this tyme.

In Leiden the studie for doctors, or as them be called phisikers, be moste faymus and arduous and MJ be in need of much payper for his notes which he doth barter from a printer in that towne, and I doth use herewithe. The master didst succeede in the Year of our Lord 1659 and doth vouwe to find his goode familie in Scotlande. The Dutchman doth advyse agaynst this foolish queste but MJ persist so the Dutchman maketh the offer to garde the master at least to London whereapon he hath business to attende with a factor, who be called Joseph Vanderhook by nayme.

Jan Martens doth advyse MJ to barter a sworde for in England all gentlemen carry the sworde as a marke of ranke. MJ doth barter a quaynt Samuri from the oriente and a brokke blayde of Damascus for the sayme purse. A blacksmithe be payd to grynde the broke blayde to a dork and a small blayde to cutte his face haire by day and also doth cutte our bodie haire. A sivlersmithe maketh the blayde into a fynne dork and a handle in silver for the small peece.

Prayse the Lord who didst bring our master to England.

Wenesday 18 June 1662

So far Jane's accounts have been plain descriptive passages and this is much the same, but already the eagerness to write her memoirs is beginning to wear off. She wrote two in each of the first two months but now they slow down to one each month. Anyone who has kept a diary will recognise this pattern. She is also developing the confidence to ask questions. Clearly the two housemaids didn't spend all their time working.

63

They discussed matters between themselves and with John over meals and at night.

Understandably the girls wanted to know more about John and his early life and how he came to be in Tyneham. We would also like to know. Surely a handsome, gifted gentleman, would have chosen to make his home in London, not in the depths of the countryside. Why did he leave Holland? After all, Amsterdam was considered to have the highest standard of living and the pinnacle of enlightened living on the Continent, above even that of London.

The Dutchman, Jan Martens, must have been a considerable influence on the much younger doctor. The boy had saved his life and he was honour bound to care for the lad. He impressed on the boy how important it was to acquire an education in order to secure a good job. Nothing has changed there. In Dutch society at that time status was measured by wealth, not class as in England. The boy was persuaded to attend school to learn Latin, and then to apply to a university to qualify in a profession. The boy was given no choice because Jan Martens decided the lad would be a physician rather than a lawyer: the most highly respected professions of the day. The boy had money to pay for his keep and tuition, from his share of the treasure.

Jan's parents had no room in their house but Jan's father had a brother living in Leiden, who had spare room as well as a son who was the same age as the young lad. The issue was resolved with or without the young boy's consent. Not that it mattered, because the boy was destined to become a polymath so it was almost irrelevant what he studied. The important point was that he would emerge with qualifications and stature.

The boy applied himself studiously, and admits that it was gruelling work, but nevertheless he enjoyed being part of a family, and was happy and contented. He obviously enjoyed the family life so much that he yearned to trace his own real family in Scotland. Jan's cousin and his parents tried to discourage this ambition, but the boy was adamant. Apart from his medical studies the young man began to take an interest in politics and philosophy and was probably well aware of the works of Hobbes, Descartes, Grotius and Spinoza.

The doctor graduated in 1659 with his ambition still intact. Jan was so concerned about the young man's safety on his fruitless quest to Scotland, that he offered to escort John to London. In fact we know that Jan was an opportunist and not beyond using the naïve doctor for his own benefit. Jan was currently 'an agent' (shipping contractor) working for a group of Amsterdam merchants. Local 'factors' (sub-contractors) in far off countries would purchase goods such as silk, spices and porcelain usually in exchange for goods produced in Holland such as grain, woollen and linen fabrics, and iron goods. Periodically this exchange got out of balance in which case the Merchants would settle the difference in bullion (usually silver). Normally the flow of cash was from London to Amsterdam but sometimes the flow was the other way (probably because a ship had sunk en-route). It was Jan's job to ensure the bullion reached its destination safely and he needed good reliable men to help him protect the valuable delivery. Jan had such a mission to a 'factor' in the City of London, by the name of Joseph Vanderhoek (I suspect the name was originally Van Der Hoek, but had been anglicised to avoid problems with the local population in case they turned zenophobic).

Before the pair set off on the short trip across the perilous North Sea, Jan suggested that John should purchase a sword, because all gentlemen wore a sword in England, because it was the customary insignia of status. I think we can be forgiven for thinking that Jan was anticipating trouble. The bullion would be the jackpot for any thief prepared to take them on in combat.

The young doctor promptly set off to find the nearest sword dealer. Although the account does not say so, we can imagine the salesman making extravagant claims about the virtues of one sword or another. Possibly in desperation he offered the doctor a hugely expensive Samuri sword imported from Japan. At this time, the Dutch had a trade monopoly with Japan so goods from the Far East would have been plentiful in Amsterdam. In other countries such goods would have been extremely rare. Obviously the low weight of this unusual sword appealed to John, who was also fascinated by the quench pattern along the steel blade. No doubt the salesman made even more extravagant claims about how sharp it was and how it could cleave a man in two with a single blow, but John didn't like the price tag. To clinch the deal the salesman offered to throw in a broken Damascus blade as well. This blade would have had an even more impressive quench pattern across the whole blade. John was hooked and made the purchase, probably with disapproval from his friend, Jan. They were supposed to be shopping for weapons not jewelery.

Undeterred, John asked a blacksmith to cut the broken blade down to dagger (dork or dirk) size, but without disturbing the quench pattern. The blacksmith had no choice but to cut it with a grindstone, which he did. The next stop was a silversmith who was persuaded to bind the handle with leather and to fix a decorative guard to the shortened blade. He also asked the same silversmith to make a hinged silver handle for the remaining small piece of blade left over (probably similar to a present day cut-throat razor). It is quite possible that John made a sketch of the handle, although the account doesn't say. Hard steel blades of this quality were extremely rare and were reputed to be able to slice through normal low quality iron swords of the day but I seriously doubt this legend. Why try to cut the sword of the enemy when you can so easily cut off the hand that holds it?

Jane's account mentions that the doctor shaved daily which was unusual at that time. His friend Jan had a luxurious beard, but John may have had difficulty growing facial hair despite having a good head of dark brown hair on his head. Some men are like that. It would not have escaped John that the Damascus blade was far better than any scalpel in his collection of medical instruments. Perhaps he intended the blade for this purpose originally. All we know is that he used it for shaving.

CHAPTER 7
The Factor

Thursday 17 July 1662

In London MJ and his friend delivereth to the factor much silver bullyon in care of a goldsmithe. The factor then maketh his house open to them as gestes.

MJ doth admyre the factor muche but thinketh nowte for London citie which be loude, withe crowdes, and uncleane and stinke with shytte afloat in the river. He sayeth before 5 years hence the citie wilt be dead of plague it be so filthie. The dead wilt be not buried if the shytte canst not be cleared. He also sayeth that vermin doth carrie the plague not mal odores or tuche. He doth intend to pruffe his fancie withe a Hygens scoppe. MJ doth admire the wisdom of the factor for maykinge his home outsyde the citie in Southwark but doth implore the factor to heede his warninge for 2 personnes in everie 3 wilt surelie die.

The factor advyseth MJ not to journie to Scotlande for it be a journie of fooles and Kings, but MJ doth Paye no heede and doth beg a horse from the stayble of the factor. In 2 days after 50 miles in the saddle in rayne MJ wast set apon by theeves, 3 in number, which vex MJ and giveth grayte angere so he doth draw forth his dork which maketh the theeves laffe at the smallness. Whereupon the master doth show the Samuri from his back and maketh a challenge to the scowndrilles. One ruffyan stryketh at MJ who didst plunge his dork in the legge of the man which mayketh the others flee in feare.

Our master be full with giltte that his angere be grayte to rob him of goode sense. His purse wast no match for his life. In this instante MJ doth see his vouwe be follie and returneth to the factor in sorrie apologie.

In goode grace the factor doth offer MJ a taske to garde silver bullyon aborde a shippe of Portugal to Venice to paye for glasse wares. Whylst he awayte the shippe MJ hast the fancie to maketh Joseph a neuwe privie withe a Delfte bowle which he doth draw on large payper for the potter in Hollande

At a coffee shoppe MJ didst evesdroppe on talk of a shippe withe 2 hulles and didst introduce himself to William Petty of the Admiraltie who giveth MJ much detaylle of the craffte, which the master doth put to payper. The master oft doth draw with a square stick of

black stuffe wrapped in payper which MJ doth say
cometh from a mynne in Borrowdayle in the north and
be called by some as plumbago.
Prayse the Lord who keepeth the master sayfe at sea.

Thursday 17 July 1662

This is the third such account about the life of John and his friends. Possibly Jane doesn't think that her life is interesting enough compared to the excitement and drama of the doctor's experiences.

Two days after they left Amsterdam, Jan and John sailed up the River Thames where their merchant ship docked at Wapping quay, in sight of London Bridge. The factor's premises were in Thames Street only a few minutes walk away, but he was on the quayside to greet them and to supervise the unloading of the cargo and to reload a fresh cargo of raw materials for the return journey. This illustrates the Dutch business model, which was based on the concept of 'middlemen finishers'. Basically the Dutch imported raw materials such as woven woollens and linens, and subjected them to finishing processes such as bleaching and dyeing to increase their value, and then re-exported them back for resale at a higher price. This was highly profitable, highly successful and elevated the Dutch economy to the highest on the Continent.

The bullion was safely transferred to a well respected and trusted goldsmith. Banks didn't exist in England, although they had banks in Holland. Goldsmiths often provided promissory notes (paper money) in exchange for gold or silver deposits. Afterwards, Joseph Vanderhoek kindly invited them to dine and spend the night at his house, outside Southwark, with his family.

Later that afternoon they were rowed across the river by a ferryman, who skilfully avoided the islands of floating faeces, to a point on the opposite bank, where they took a short stroll up to the large, substantial, brick built house of the factor (the site is now beneath the railway tracks at London Bridge station). Clearly, his was a job that paid very well.

After dinner in friendly discussion John made it clear that he could not live in the city. Despite the many fine buildings and palaces, and despite the wealth and prosperity, the city was too big and there were too many people. It was noisy, unclean, unhealthy and it stank. It was an impeding disaster and he predicted that the plagued would strike within five years. John even congratulated Joseph for having the wisdom to live amongst the green fields. He implored that neither Joseph nor his family nor his servants should venture into the city when the plague arrives.

Joseph queried his prediction and John explained his reasoning. Just over fifty years ago Amsterdam fell victim to the plague, but it is a clean, well ordered city and successfully used quarantine to stop the plague becoming an epidemic, Even so, many thousands died. London is many times bigger, unclean and disorganised. When the plague arrives it will soon become an epidemic: 'the dead wilt be not buried if the shytte canst not be cleared'. Unburied bodies will increase the spread of the disease. Two in every three will die (a previous outbreak in 1347 killed about 60% of the population).

The doctor also pointed out that the current wisdom was that the plague was carried by bad odours or contact with an infected person. The doctor disagreed.

Since the wind changes direction almost daily, then the disease would be spread in all directions, but that did not happened in practice. Secondly, human contact didn't necessarily transmit the disease. Not all members of a family under quarantine caught the disease: many did but some didn't. Some of the family died of starvation because they we unable to leave the house under quarantine. It would seem that humans carried the disease from place to place, and country to country, but it was his opinion that the real culprits were vermin (fleas and lice). He could not prove his theory yet, but he intended to obtain a 'Huygens scope' (microscope) in order to confirm his belief by examining these creature found on an infected person and on a healthy person. If there was a difference then this would be conclusive proof.

In 1663 (three years later) the plague hit Amsterdam again, and two years later the Black Death reached London, just as John predicted. The results were devastating. The doctor did not acquire his first microscope until after the great fire of London in 1666 even though Hooke had published his microscopic observations in the 'Micrographia' a year earlier.

John also told Joseph of his intended quest to trace his ancestors in Scotland. Joseph and Jan Martens were both dismayed and did their best to politely discourage the doctor in this foolhardy adventure. He had no name, no date of birth and no place of birth. Moreover, Joseph pointed out that only Kings and fools undertake such a long, perilous journey that far north, and in his view the doctor was neither. John pointed out that he was honour bound to undertake the pilgrimage because he had vowed to do so.

Joseph was obviously impressed. Here was a highly educated and knowledgable gentleman who was prepared to risk his life to honour a vow.

Joseph was a much travelled and well seasoned businessman and must have known that the 350 mile journey would take at least three weeks in the saddle, assuming there were no mishaps on the way. Perhaps he was testing the doctor's resolve.

As it happened, it rained heavily for two days and in this time John only covered fifty miles and probably spent two nights in uncomfortable coaching inns with bad food. On the third day he was beset by three scoundrels who demanded his purse. There was barely enough money to reach Scotland and back, which was hardly worth risking his life for. What angered John most was that it would mean the end of his quest, so he stood his ground and drew his dagger.

The three ruffians laughed in derision and asked if that was his sword, so John drew the Samuri from his back to show them he was better armed. The bravest of the ruffians tried to strike John but he parried the blow and stabbed the fool in the thigh, whereapon the other two ran off.

John had never experienced real anger before and realised it was a dangerous emotion because it robbed him of logical thought. He should never have risked his life for such a paltry sum. It finally dawned on him that he should never have made his vow either. His quest was an impossible fools errand. Reason prevailed and he promptly returned to the house of Joseph Vanderhoek, where he apologised for his stupidity.

Like Jan Martens, Joseph was not beyond taking advantage of this situation for his own benefit. He gracefully accepted the apology and was glad to see the doctor had come to no harm and had come to his senses. He then propositioned the doctor to undertake a task for him in the spring of 1660, for which he would be well rewarded. In the meantime he was welcome to stay at his house because his children adored the doctor and his exciting tales. Joseph asked the doctor to accompany some bullion to Venice to pay his factor there for a valuable cargo of Venetian glassware.

There is a strong possibilty that Joseph's activities as a private merchant were unknown to his own principals in Amsterdam. Perhaps he was doing some under-the-counter business on the side. The reason that I mention this is because it transpired that Joseph had hired a Portuguese ship to make the journey. Surely he would have hired a Dutch vessel normally used by his principals. It was also possible that Joseph was financing the operation with some of the bullion that John had brought with him. This is all speculation and we will never know the truth. John certainly didn't suspect anything.

The following day Joseph had a business meeting at a nearby coffee house and invited the doctor to join him. While Joseph haggled over the price of various goods, John evesdropped on the surrounding conversations. One gentleman was explaining to another the virtues of twin hulled vessels: they were more stable, less likely to heel, were faster and were less dependant on wind direction when lateen rigged. This information obviously rang a bell for John because he was often grounded waiting for the wind to change. He politely interrupted the conversation and introduced himself as John Leiden, physician from Amsterdam. One of the two men acknowledged the doctor and announced that he was William Petty of the Admiralty.

John explained that he had already been shipwrecked twice, which explained his interest in their conversation. Mr Petty (soon to be knighted Sir William Petty and Fellow of the Royal Society) told him of his plan to build an experimental twin hulled boat to be launched in Dublin the following year, and described the little boat in detail. Joseph had finished his business so the doctor politely begged his leave.

While waiting for a favourable wind the doctor designed a new privy for Joseph to order from Delft. I suspect that the doctor felt guilty about imposing on Joseph's hospitality and intended the new privy as a gift. He also drew a design for a catamarran based on the proportions that he gleaned from William Petty. Jane notes that the doctor often made drawings with a square drawing stick (pencil) made from black stuff (pure graphite from a mine near Borrowdale in present day Cumbria).

CHAPTER 8
The boat

Saturday 16 August 1662

We asketh at bed and the master doth tell us the manner of his visite to Dorset and the buildinge of his boat. At the barter at Chatham MJ didst succeede to two Doreys 4 rods longe and didst barter with Nathan Salter of Swanwich to tayke and ajoyne the 2 craffte at his yard accordinge to the manner that MJ hath drew on payper.

MJ hath nowte silver left so he doth seeke a loane with the factor to reward master Salter by month for 6 months untille the craffte be builted and the werke be done. MJ hath a bagge of jewelles to sette down lest he be not ayble to paye the factor. After the jewelles be valued the factor taketh alone but one emeralde. The factor doth also advyse MJ to fille his craffte with cork lest it be sunke lyke alle shippes.

Master Salter tayketh MJ and the 2 Dorys to Swanwich
and beginneth werke whylst MJ doth return by fish boat
into London for to sayle to Venice.

Thanks be to the goode Lord who didst keep the master
sayfe into Venice.

Saturday 16 August 1662

The next memoir tells us more about the obsessive nature of the doctor. Perhaps obsessive is a little unfair. He was certainly determined and highly focussed and applied himself with zeal to whatever was the cuurent project on his mind, and wouldn't let go at any cost. Although his quest to Scotland was an abject failure, he was not deterred. He now embarks on another risky venture.

John must have been hugely impressed by his chance meeting with William Petty because he saw this idea as the best way of travelling around in safety. Nowadays we have the motor car for personal mobility, but the principle was the same for a small boat at that time, and just as desirable.

In terms of risk, John was not to know that a gentleman called John Aubrey on the Isle of Wight had exactly the same idea and launched his vessel in 1663. Unknown to the doctor his chances of success were balanced in his favour. Likewise the first vessel designed by William Petty was also successful, although he was not so fortunate with later vessels.

Apart from some high winds and the odd storm, the winter of 1660 was remarkably mild, which allowed John to pursue his current venture. In terms of capital John had some money and a handful of poorly cut and polished jewels (his share of the stolen treasure), which included a very large emerald. Regardless of his requirement for personal transport he obviously did not intend to bankrupt himself.

I think we can assume that John showed his friend Joseph some drawings of his boat design. Joseph was not a naval architect and was unable to make any useful comment, except perhaps to ask what made this design better than existing boats. Probably as far as he could see if it got into difficulties it would sink just as easily as any other boat. They only had William Petty's assumption that it had superior handling and was faster. Perhaps it would be safer if the two hulls were filled with cork. At least it could not sink and would give the crew a better chance of surving. We know that it was a suggestion from Joseph because Jane's account tells us so. We have no clue what inspired John to select pumice rather than cork. We only know that later John built a house with pumice as thermal insulation. Pumice was known and had been widely used since Roman times, so John would have been aware of its unusual properties.

John had two immediate problems: obtaining two convenient hulls and finding a suitable boatyard to join them together. There were countless small boatyards along the Thames and around the south coast, building and reapairing small fishing boats and rowing boats. It is quite posssible that John went scouting some local yards along the Thames and perhaps they re-directed him to the Navy dockyards at Chatham. The Navy often had to transport people bewteen ships at sea and many ships carried a 'Jolly' boat or 'Dorey' for this purpose.

The Navy periodically sold off surplus equipment usually by auction and Jane's account tells us that this is where John purchased two slim Dorys each 4 rods long (22 feet). It was at this auction that John met Nathan Salter, a boat builder from Swanwich (Swanage) on the Dorset coast, and during casual conversation discussed what John intended to do with the two craft, no doubt trying to secure a contract, even to the point of offering to tow the craft to his boatyard.

We don't know anything about Nathan Salter and whether he was short of money, but he was certainly keen to build John's craft. Unfortunately his price was beyond John's purse. Undeterred, John approached Joseph and asked for a loan, using his small purse of jewels as security. The wily Dutchman agreed to have the jewels valued and if they proved of any value he would advance a loan. We don't know what the valuation was, but we do know from Jane's account that he only took the large emerald and made the loan in full.

John begged leave of Joseph for a week to accompany Nathan and his two boats to the yard in Swanwich and to finalize a contract. Once again we don't know the details, but we know that the builder was paid by Joseph at the end of each month during the six month build. During this time, John would be on his voyage to Venice, and I think we can assume that Joseph was a difficult paymaster and would need to be assured that the money was well spent before parting with any more.

Something must have happened on this trip to Swanwich that tempted John to stay in England and make his home at Tyneham close to Swanwich. Perhaps it was the beautiful uncrowded countryside, the very mild weather for this time of year, the closeness of the sea, the isolation. Perhaps he was made an offer to build a house that he couldn't refuse, or he could have felt guilty about staying with the Vanderhoek family for so long. We will never know and Jane's account gives no clues.

My own view is that the doctor had already experienced family life with the cousin of Jan Martens and obviously liked the family feeling. I think he experienced the same with the Vanderhoek family but could not accept living in London just to be near them. Now that he had a boat of his own, Joseph and his family were within easy reach. At that time a day's journey by boat would have been considered 'within easy reach'. Clearly people in those days had much more patience than nowadays.

The choice of Tyneham as a place to build his house may seem strange, but I suspect that the doctor looked for a place to keep his boat that was close to his house and close to the ship yard for maintenance and repairs. Worbarrow bay is the first bay travelling west from Swanwich that has a direct path to a nearby village (Tyneham). Basically, Tyneham ticks all the boxes.

Holland at that time was well organized, clean and affluent and well regulated. I believe that what attracted the yound doctor to England was the lack of regulation, the chaotic free-for-all to do as he pleased. Holland was also engaged in almost perpetual religious wars with various factions across Europe, whereas the English had settled this problem during its civil war. Peace reigned and allowed the population to go about the business of making money. England was also an island nation with a strong navy to protect it, whereas Holland had only recently won its freedom from Spain and shared its borders with other powerful nations.

CHAPTER 9
Venice

Friday 12 September 1662

The master doth tell to us this tayle in the pharma withe a mappe apon the wall so that we shalt hath goode understandinge of his visite to Venice in the year of our Lord 1660 in the month of April.

On syte of the shippe MJ was moste awed in its smallness as it be a caravel of Portugal and he spayke to the captayne in that tonge who sayeth the shippe hath quickeness and doth ryde well. In Lizbon the shippe doth stay for water and vittals and trayde and at Messina for lemons. At Ragussa, which citie be at war withe Turkes, the master of the harbore asketh wherefrom art thou comest hither and whereto goest thou and art thou Christian. A priest cometh aborde and spake withe MJ in the Latin and barter withe powder which killeth alle mytes and small animules. MJ doth see withe his own eye that this be true and be moste in awe. MJ doth barter the priest 20 silver shillings for 1 barrel of powder in hopes it wilt yield 5 tymes more in England and doth promise the pryce of 10 barrels more.

The factor in Venice hath the name Giovanni Cellini of Murano who be in dismay by the tardie shippe for a plague of flyinge animules be nye apon them. This gentleman doth witness the powder werke and doth offer 100 silver for the barrel. After the bargayne be struck the factor doth say that twice the silver be still a bargayne for the powder be known as Persyan which be most precious.

The shippe doth sayle agayne to Ragussa after loadinge glasse wares but MJ hath not 200 silver for the 10 barrels promised. The goode captayne taketh 1 barrel and MJ doth barter his precious dork for 4 barrels if the harbore master doth agree on paper withe seals to sell 50 barrels by the year to MJ alone and no other.

In Messina the captayne doth barter his barrel for 80 silver and be moste pleased and bringeth the shippe to London in alle promptness in the year of our Lord 1660 in the month of October.

The master taketh small partes of a barrel and doth barter withe apothecaries these partes shoppe by shoppe in the citie tille a barrel be sold in a week for

200 silver which much pleased Joseph and MJ. The factor desireth to be a partner withe MJ. In the mean Joseph advyseth MJ to rayse the pryce to maketh his barrels last tille next year. In the mean tyme MJ doth collect pumyce from wynne factors in the citie for his boat and doth sayle in a fish boat bound for Devon to collect his neuwe boat at Swanwich.

Prayse be to the Lord who didst keep our master sayfe at sea.

Friday 12 September 1662

Once again the inspiration for this memoir was probably one of the doctor's geography lessons for the girls, which he delivered in his surgery with a map on the wall. It signifies the emergence of John as a businessman as he comes under the influence of his Dutch friends and the free-for-all commerce and enterprise atmosphere of the period.

John was surprised that the Portuguese caravel was so small compared to a Dutch merchantman, but according to the captain it was fast and manoeuvrable, which was a wise precaution to avoid corsairs off the Barbary coast. It must have been a surprise to Joseph that John spoke Portuguese: he had obviously chosen his agent well.

The ship called at Lisbon to trade fabrics and iron and to take on provisions and water and at Messina (for lemons and trade), and again at Ragussa (Dubrovnik). At that time, the Republic of Ragussa was a city state under the protection of the more powerful city state of Venice who were at war with the Ottoman Empire over control of the island of Crete. This would account for the ship being met by a priest (interpreter) and the harbour master who demanded to know if they were Christian, where they from and what cargo they were carrying. While the official consulted with his superiors for permission for the ship to dock, John engaged the priest in conversation (in Latin).

During their talk, the priest tried to sell John a pouch of white powder which he claimed could kill flies. When John put it to the test, it really worked. The priest also confirmed that the powder killed all insects. John asked where the powder came from and the priest waved his hand towards the mountains and replied that the flowers grew everywhere. John then pointed to a barrel and asked how much would it cost to fill the barrel if he paid in silver shillings (the only currency he had). The priest took a shilling (to assay the silver content) and came back later with a price of 20 silver shillings for a barrel. John was certain that the barrel held at least 100 or possibly 200 pouches which he was certain he could sell for at least a shilling each. It was an offer he could not refuse, even though it emptied his money belt.

The priest told him that he could supply many more barrels and John agreed to purchase ten more barrels on his return from Venice. The priest could supply no more because he had no more barrels, but still plenty of powder. This gamble probably made him very nervous and disturbed his sleep. He had no more money left with which to pay.

The ship entered the Venice lagoon at the beginning of July and they headed north to the island of Murano where they met the local factor, Giovanni Cellini. The factor was agitated because the ship was so late and 'the season of insects' was due any moment. While the ship began loading the precious cargo of glassware,

John asked the factor about the plague of insects that appear every year, and told him of the barrel of powder he had. Giovanni already knew of a powder from Persia, but it was so expensive that few could afford to use it. The wealthy people of Venice vacated the city during July and August to avoid insect bites. Casually he asked John the cost of his powder when John demonstrated how potent it was. John pretended reluctance to sell, but eventually agreed a price of 100 silver shillings. After the deal, Giovanni admitted he could re-sell it for more than twice that price. John now had half the money he needed. It was an expensive lesson in the art of barter.

Fortunately, the Portuguese captain was prepared to pay for one barrel, because had had seen the doctor make quick money in Venice. This still left the doctor with the problem of paying for the remaining four barrels. The only item of value that John possessed was the Damascus dagger which was worth considerably more than four barrels. If he parted with his dagger he wanted the remaining barrels and exclusive trade in the powder.

After much haggling the priest drew up two contracts on vellum in very poor Latin, signed by the doctor, the harbour master, the captain and the priest. The contract gave him exclusive rights to trade the powder at 1000 shillings or equivalent silver for 50 barrels minimum per year provide he supplied the barrels or similar measures. The doctor added his seal and said that a ship would call at this time every year and the captain would present the contract or his seal to verify his authority to collect the powder.

John had made his very first deal as a merchant and if all went well he now had an income of at least 5000 shillings per year and possibly a lot more. He regretted having to part with his dagger, but at least he still had the small razor and he would be able to redeem his emerald and honour his debt to Joseph, to say nothing of being able to buy a house. To my knowledge this contract and its copy no longer exist.

On the return journey the captain sold his barrel in Messina for the equivalent of 80 shillings, which pleased him immensely. The ship arrived back in London in late October 1660.

According to Jane's account, John spent a week walking the streets of the city selling small stoneware jars of his powder to every Apothecary he could find. By the end of the week he had sold half a barrel for twice the money he expected. Word soon got around that a new cure for fleas and lice was on sale and within a few days the rest of the barrel was sold.

Joseph was hugely impressed with the profit margin and introduced John to the economic principle of supply and demand. At this rate John's supply would run out before he could obtain a fresh supply from Ragussa. He suggested that John should increase the price to reduce the demand and make even more profit. He also wanted to be in on the deal for the next consignment. There had to be a market for the powder in Holland too.

John acquired a quantity of pumice from a wine dealer who used it as cargo packing, and then paid a fisherman from Devon to take him and his pumice to Swanwich to collect his boat.

CHAPTER 10
The blacksmith

Munday 20 October 1662

Mary didst complayne to the master and me withe her that the kitchen pump be growse efforte and taketh much tyme to fille the butte in the roofe and and doth leeke from the leather pype. In tyme the Jake Glover the blacksmithe of Wareham, in the companie of the master after a shooe be made for the horse, doth visite to assay the pump and declareth the leather flaps insyde be broke. On this tyme I taketh leave to serve pottage, bread and ale for alle, withe the plezure of the master implore them to mayketh a better pump and pype.

The master hath goode reasoninge for better flaps and joynts that leeke not and doth challenge the blacksmithe to mayketh a sleeve of brass which slyde outsyde a pype of brass half waye, and in the other half another pype with a pinne and slotte to lock them as one as a French bayonette.

The master doth say the leather flaps be of nowte sense by reason that they be insyde the pump and sayeth a brass ball atop a lether ring lasteth longer and must be outsyde the pump. The blacksmithe wast much in awe of the neuwe methode and laffte aloude and praysed the master as a genius for a reaon so simple. Jake doth see the methode in an instante and hayste away to mayketh suche but the master doth stay his hand to tayketh more ale and dinner and doth prayse me well later for the goode foode at tayble. The master doth confess that Jake hath a quicke mynde and wilt mayke goode werkes betwixt them. For he sayeth that the future wealth of alle England be in yron and the manner of werkinge it. I carest not for such matters but I be in neede of a neuwe pump.

Prayse the Lord for a goode harvest for alle.

Munday 20 October 1662

The next memoir indicates that the two girls are becoming accustomed to running the house and concerns everyday problems that they experienced, rather than writing reminiscences of the doctor.

The memoir begins to explain how the doctor intended to expanded his capacity to develop his ideas. To his credit, the doctor realised that iron was the metal of the future but mankind needed to improve the ways they worked the metal and so did he. He also appreciated that wood still had an important place, but again man needed to improve his processing methods to make best use of its properties. Lastly, he was aware that progress required an ever increasing degree of accuracy and specialisation to meet the demands of new technology. His intent was put these three concepts at his fingertips.

It is unlikely that Jane appreciated the doctor's vision of the future enough to have written about it. Two other memoirs follow this one along the same lines. Clearly the doctor was setting up the infra structure in terms of skilled craftsmen to put his ideas into practice.

What is most likely to have inspired Jane to write this memoir is that she personally knew the blacksmith.

Wareham was only a tiny village so everybody knew everyone else. He had also come to fix the problem with the pump that filled up the water butts in the roof. Both she and Mary faced this task every day, so for them it was a pressing problem.

On a technical note, blacksmiths generally worked with iron, although many knew how to work brass too. In those days iron ore was melted in furnaces and then cast into moulds (cast iron). This iron is fine under compression but has no tensile strength and is very brittle (it would crack if it was hit with a hammer). The cast iron was then smelted and stirred with wooden poles to remove the slag and reduce the carbon content and finally poured into ingots (pure iron). This iron was very weak and soft, but blacksmiths could hardened it by heating in a forge and then hammering and quenching in water (wrought iron) with properties similar to but not as good as modern mild steel.

Wrought iron had a thousand and one uses: horseshoes, door hinges, door locks, garden tools, kitchen utensils, cooking pots, knives, cutlery, lamps, candle holders, wheel axles and so on. Not much has changed. The Industrial Revolution didn't occur for another century, but when it did arrive it was based on iron and the technology to work it.

Plumbing at that time did not exist. The doctor's house was very rare in that respect because he did have some rudimentary plumbing made of brass pipe. Pipes of lead were more common and had been used since Roman times, because it was easy to work. Foundries were able to cast iron or brass pipes, but they were of poor quality and only produced in short lengths. These cast pipes were very heavy and hugely expensive. An alternative method for brass was also available, in which short lengths (three feet) were rolled from flat sheet brass with a soldered the seam. One end was usually swaged wider than other end so that two pipes could be slotted together with a solder or putty joint. John's house was equipped with this type of pipe, which obviously worked well enough.

Jane's account begins with the arrival of the doctor and the blacksmith, Jake Glover from Wareham. The two had ridden back together after Jake had made and fitted John's horse with a new shoe. It seems that Jake was also a farrier. Jake was in good spirits, probably because the doctor had struck a deal with him to pay for his time to make the journey, although we don't know this for sure.

They went to the pump in the garden where Jane was asked to join them to explain the problem with pumping water. All credit to Jane for speaking up and pointing out that the garden pump was not the problem: it had always been good and reliable. The problem was the kitchen force pump (stirrup pump). A wooden bucket had to be filled at the garden pump and carried into the kitchen. A flexible leather pipe connected to the force pump was put into the bucket. Another leather pipe at the other end of the pump was connected to the brass pipe that filled the water butts in the roof. This joint leaked badly, moreover it was difficult to use the pump and it took a long time to fill the butts.

Jake inspected the force pump and announced that the leather flap valves inside were no longer working properly which accounted for the long time that it took to fill the butts. The reason why it required so much effort was because they were pumping water so high up to the roof.

The doctor asked Jake if he was prepared to make a replacement pump of a better design. At first Jake was reluctant to take on the challenge, but Jane interrupted and invited them both to join her at lunch: broth and fresh bread with pewter tankards of ale. During lunch Jane explained how important it was to get this problem resolved.

After lunch Jake listened to the doctor. This is the first glimpse we have of the doctor's analytical skills. The pump itself was not the problem. John was certain that Jake could make a simple piston and cylinder. The root of the problem was the flap valve or to be more precise, both of the flap valves inside the pump. The next problem was to devise a simple method of connecting pipes together in a leak-proof joint. It didn't matter what the pipes were made of, it was the joint that was important.

The doctor sketched with a graphite pencil on a piece of paper what he had in mind for the joint. To his credit

Jake grasped the principle immediately. Not only that, but he also understood what it meant for him in practice: mainly that the idea did not need accurate tolerances in order to remain leak-proof. He also realised that the doctor would need at least a dozen of these joints for his house. This was a business proposition that was worth pursuing.

As Jane describes it, the joint consisted of a brass sleeve, slightly larger than a brass pipe. A pipe was inserted into the sleeve half way and soldered in position. The other piece of pipe has a steel pin soldered in the end so that the ends of the pin protruded. The sleeve had two slots cut in the ends that engaged with this pin. One or more leather discs with a hole in the centre (washers) were placed in the sleeve and then the two pipes were squeezed together and given a slight twist to lock them. Nowadays we would call this a bayonet fitting. It was leak-proof because of the compression of the leather washers and not because of the flatness and accuracy of the two mating pipe ends or how well they fitted the sleeve.

We have no indication that the doctor could read Arabic, so it unlikely that he got the idea from Al Jazari who invented a bayonet fitting candle holder in the 13th century. It is much more likely that he knew how military bayonets were fitted to muskets used by the French Army of the time.

Jake was fired up and wanted to know what the doctor had in mind for the flap valves. The doctor explained that putting the valves inside the pump was wrong. The valves were working parts that could wear out or go wrong, in which case they needed to be replaced or repaired. This was impossible if they were inside. The piston and cylinder provided the force to move the water around which they would do regardless of how well they fitted. In other words, accuracy was not essential. Accuracy made the pump work more efficiently, but what determined if the pump worked at all were the flap valves (one way check valves).

The design of the valves was crucial and needed to be improved. If the valves were in the pipes instead of in the pump, then the feed pipe and the outflow pipe could both be at the bottom. This would mean the girls would be pushing downwards in order to push the water up to the butts. Pushing down is much easier than lifting upwards.

The doctor then sketched a simple valve with a ball inside that seated on a leather disk at one end and a metal pin at the other. When the flow of water pushed the ball against the leather washer the water flow was cut off. In the other direction the ball was pushed against the pin allowing the water to continue to flow. Jake laughed out load and exclaimed that he would never have thought of such a simple device. He declared that the doctor was a gentleman and a genius.

The doctor must have been impressed that Jake had grasped the principle so quickly without further explanation. There was much more to Jake than a big man with a hammer: he had brains too. Jake was so keen to get started that he begged leave, but the doctor insisted that he stay for more ale and dinner.

Jane tells us that the doctor was very happy that night and praised her for suggesting lunch at just the right moment. The doctor confirmed that he was looking for an intelligent metal worker and he was convinced that he found one in Jake. Jane would have been inwardly pleased at the compliment and even more pleased that the pump issue would soon be resolved.

Normally servants didn't complain, but the girls must be gaining in confidence enough to have complained about the pump as this account demonstrates. Perhaps the doctor's views on equality were finally penetrating the inhibitions of his two housemaids, or should we say mistresses.

It would have been most unusual for servants to complain, but it was also most unusual to outwardly treat them as equals. We should give the doctor credit for his views on social equality, but also credit for responding quickly to the girls when they did complain.

My personal view is that Jane has assumed the mantle of house manager whereas Mary is content with being 'eye candy', although to be fair Mary is also the most outspoken, leaving Jane in the background to observe. Considering they are sharing the same lover, they seem to have developed a remarkably well adjusted relationship.

CHAPTER 11
The carpenter

Tewsday 11 November 1662

In a shorte tyme the blacksmithe calleth again with a new yron pump which be so smoothe and be less efforte and hath no needes for buckets in the kitchen for a neuwe pype be layed to the welle outsyde and doth leeke nowte from the brass ends or the leather pype. Maryand me be moste pleased and keepeth the pump asyde the wash tub but not in the pantrie as before.

The wether hast been unkynde withe much rayne and maketh Mary complayne of the wetness. Methinks she doth complayne oft and the master may become displeased.

Withe Jake be the carpenter, Alan Rutland or Rutty as he be called, to witness the neuwe brass ends withe balls insyde. Twas Rutty who advysed Jake to polish the balles in a barrel withe sand and water while rollinge.

Rutty also bringeth us rayne covers which the master doth call French parapluey mayde by 6 stickes of beech woode lyke a cart wheele covered withe a yard of sayle clothe cutte by the Sire of Mary, with a sticke in the midst to uphold the cover aloft so that the pluey doth keep us dry. In 2 days Rutty doth come agayne withe another pluey which canst be locked withe a twist and fold away and be much impruffed.

Mistress Price bringeth curtains, muslins, linen tayble cloths, and divers dresses in such numbers that she hath a boy and a cart to ayde her. Edwin, the boy, canst not speake so the master doth look in his throate to assay his infirms and telleth the boy to eat seaweed. There be so mennie petticotes and suche in my dressinge room that I canst ware a neuwe petticoate by the day for a weeke and there be nowte room for more.

Mary spayke withe the boy in synnes of the hand and she pleadeth with the master to grant the boy werke withe the animals. The master sayeth we hath nowte room but the boy canst laybore by the day for a half silver each day and eat goode foode with us alle.

Later the Madam of Edwin calleth by the house and prayseth the master withe tears and goode words for the grant of werke for her sonne.

On the morrow Mary doth telle me that her bed warminge vigore maketh her body tremble and luz her senses. Methinks that she doth tayke a gallon of seede from the poor master for the favore to Edwin.

The master be all of a dither and much vexed for the sayftie of Mary and me whylst he be at sea to Antwerp to meet Jan Martens and garde much silver to the factor in London. The master wast intent to sayle his boat but Joseph hath feare for it be smalle withe goodes so hye in value so MJ doth sayle in a merchantman.

The goode Lord be praysed and keepth sayfe our master into Antwerp.

Tewsday 11 November 1662

This account was written a month after the previous memoir. Again It is not so much about the doctor and his plans, but more about the two housemaids and their everyday problems with running the house. The awe and wonder of the doctor's travels and business activities is wearing off, and normal everyday life is taking over.

What interested Jane about the doctor's association with the carpenter, Alan Rutland, the neighbour of Jake the blacksmith, was the fact that he made two parasols for the girls. Apparently it was a particularly wet month and the girls were fed up with getting soaked every time they went outside to attend to the animals. Mary even went as far as suggesting to the doctor that they should have extra help with the animals.

According to this account the new force pump in the kitchen worked extremely well. They no longer had to refill the bucket because a pipe had been laid between the kitchen and the well. Jane does not tell us who did this work. The new brass valves and fittings also worked, and instead of keeping the pump in the pantry, they now left it permanently connected beside the stone wash-tub because it didn't leak any more.

Apparently, at the suggestion of 'Rutty' (the carpenter), the tiny balls in the check valves were made by putting the rough cast balls into a small barrel with fine sand and water, and then rotating the barrel to reduce them to the right size and to polish them. It seems that John's idea to hasten progress by collective 'brain storming' was beginning to work.

The girls complaints about the never ending rain and bad weather, probably inspired John to collaborate with the carpenter to make umbrellas for the girls. Parasols had been used by the Chinese and Indian cultures for millennia. They were also fashionable in France at the time. Indeed the French had two versions: the *parasol* as a sun shade and the *parapluie* as a rain shade. John was not inventing something new.

The first design was made by the carpenter and consisted of a central wooden hub with six dowel holes into which he secured six thin beech-wood sticks to form a hexagon about a yard across. This geometry would have been the easiest to make because starting with a circle of half a yard radius and keeping the drawing dividers the same, then the circumference can be marked exactly in six equal portions. Mary's father (the sail-maker) cut and hem-stitched a piece of sail cloth with little pockets at the corners to seat the ends of the sticks. An upright stick was then forced into a hole in the hub as a handle.

The second design was much more like a present day umbrella in that it was collapsible and probably used the new bayonet fitting principle because Jane mentions it was locked in position with a slight twist. The covers could also be exchanged for sun shades made of white linen with lace edges made by Mrs Price, the seamstress from Steeple. Jane doesn't give us any further details. Except that it was much improved on the first version.

The doctor's business ventures were obviously prospering because the girls were constantly making additions to the house furnishings and their wardrobes. Mrs Price made drapes for the windows and muslin curtains, as well as table cloths in linen and new dresses for the girls. Indeed, Jane tells us that they have enough to wear a different dress for each day of the week. On one occasion Mrs Price had so much to deliver that she employed a local lad with a hand cart to carry the load.

It is interesting that Jane never mentions hats or head wear in any of her memoirs. Poor folk didn't have hats so the girls would not have developed the habit of wearing head coverings except in church of a Sunday. I suspect they wore simple bonnets in church and most likely heavy knitted head covers and scarves in winter time that also covered the ears. The girls only visited London twice so they were not in a position to observe what fashionable women were or were not wearing. If anything, the girls themselves were leading fashion, at least locally. Unlike most people the girls bathed and washed their hair daily. They also had an ample supply of ribbons and laces and probably decorated their hair with these and had no need of hats .Likewise there is no mention of make-up. Queen Elizabeth I was notorious for the quantity of make-up that she used to hide her blemishes and wrinkles, but the two girls were young, attractive and healthy and didn't need make-up and like hats, they never acquired the habit.

Jane doesn't tell us how old Edwin was, only that he could not speak. The doctor even examined the lad and suggested the boy should eat seaweed. Perhaps the boy had an enlarged thyroid gland that affected his voice box or perhaps he had a growth of some sort. We will never know. Jane only tells us that Mary took a liking to the boy, Edwin, and that the boy 'spoke' by making signs with his hands. Mary pleaded with the doctor to take on the boy to help with the animals.

The doctor resisted at first on the grounds that they had no spare room, but Mary argued that the boy could just come each day as a day labourer. Finally the doctor agreed, but as usual he insisted that the girls should dust, clean and bathe the boy (to remove fleas and lice). He agreed to pay the boy six pence per day (which was more than the normal rate at the time) and that he could work seven days a week because animals need tending every day. To us this may sound a harsh deal, but to the lad at time it must have seemed like heaven had arrived. The doctor also insisted that the boy should take breakfast and lunch with them every day, including the seaweed diet.

The following day the boy's mother came to thank the doctor for his generosity. The woman was in tears of gratitude. When you are at the bottom of the poverty pit, gratitude is about the only thing you can still give. Mary too expressed her gratitude because she tells Jane the following day that her 'bed warming vigour maketh her body to tremble and lose her senses', which hardly needs translating. No doubt Mary found the task of tending and feeding the animals was arduous work and was glad to get it off her back.

There is no further mention of the animals in Jane's memoirs which suggests that Edwin was doing his job very well indeed. He did all the work and the doctor paid the bills and Mary sat about looking pretty. No doubt the doctor soon realized the real value of the work that Edwin was doing and paid him accordingly. Probably the doctor spoke to Edwin from time to time about ordering feed and bedding for the horse and winter sillage for the cows but otherwise they left everything in Edwin's capable hands.

The doctor had been asked by Joseph Vanderhoek, on a previous trip to London, to visit Antwerp to meet Jan Martens to collect some bullion. It is possible that Joseph and Jan had a business deal involving large quantities of Dalmatian powder. Normally bullion transfers were made between London and Amsterdam, so why would this one be made from Antwerp unless Joseph or Jan or both didn't want anyone knowing about it? The doctor was an ideal go-between because he was not connected directly in any way with the Dutch business. This is entirely speculative and we will never know the truth.

John was confident enough to sail his boat to Antwerp but Joseph was apprehensive about risking the bullion on such a small boat. John eventually made the trip on a merchantman in early November (the same time as Jane wrote this account). She mentions that John was very agitated and concerned about leaving the girls alone.

CHAPTER 12
Christmas

Wenesday 31 December 1662

A fulle afore the festival of Christ Mass by a weeke we hath much foode in store. The master doth barter a goose and a caypon and caskes of malmsey and ale. The master sayeth in London the river be frozen up to the bridge. The wether here be so bitter that we keepeth the poltrie in linens in the stayble and few fowkes didst attend the church for prayer on the Eve.

On the morrow we arose at dawn in thrille and fluste., At morninge tayble there be a canvas sute, lether boots, and a woolle top coat for Edwin who doth weepe with delyte as do we. After we bayke bread tis the time for MJ to fetch the poltrie and thence the pluvia before dressinge. To our delyte the master hath sette neuwe petticotes on the bed and hath mayde a blayze in the heath in the Grayte Halle so it be warme and cheerfulle.

In that instant a cart cometh to the door and it be the Sire and Madam of Mary which mayketh her so gaye.

Then in a tryce another cart cometh withe my Sire and Madam which doth mayke me joyfulle.

At the tayble there be foode aplentie and malmsey and ale for alle which maketh everie bodie gaye and of goode cheere. The master doth propose a toaste not for the King but for me and Mary, and giveth us each a giftte of an emeralde on a gold neck chayne. Tis a fortune. It be the moste best gyftte from our dearest master.

The master doth then open his house to his gestes to see the wonders therein. The Madames sayeth it be so cleene and hath envie of the water in pypes. Before darkness doth falle the carts cometh agayne and tayketh our families. MJ cutteth by halfes the caypon and mayketh a giftte to his gestes for the morrow.

Mary and me be myndefulle of such a day of thrille that we shalt be together the giftte that nytte for the plezure of the master.

We prayse the Lord for such a goode year.

Wenesday 31 December 1662

This is the first Christmas that the two girls have spent in the doctor's house. It is a touching account, made more so by the surprise arrival of their parents to share it with them. Clearly the doctor thought a great deal of the two girls judging by the fabulous pendant necklaces that he bought for them. The girls wore enough around their necks to provide a lifetime of comfort. They could walk away and live in luxury for the rest of their lives.

For a week before Christmas the girls excitedly prepared the house for the coming festivities. The doctor had purchased a goose and a capon, as well as more than the usual quantity of vegetables. He also acquired a small cask of Malmsey and a cask of ale. The pantry could barely hold the extra provisions.

It was bitterly cold so the poultry was wrapped in linen and stored, with the ale and cheese in the stable. The doctor told them that the river Thames was almost frozen over beyond London Bridge on his visit to collect the wine and presents. Despite their clamour he kept the secret of their presents. On Christmas Eve they attended St Mary's Church next door but the bitter weather kept many folk away.

The girls rose excitedly at dawn. Edwin joined them for breakfast and John presented him with a new canvas suit, strong boots of leather and a thick woollen top coat and then sent him home for the day. The boy's tears said all that could be said with the voice. The girls both cried with happiness. After breakfast while the girls baked fresh bread, John fetched the poultry from the stable.

Once the dinner was in the oven the three showered and prepared to dress. There were squeals of delight as the girls discovered that the doctor had set out new dresses for them. They went down to the Great Hall where a blazing wood fire greeted them. Almost immediately a horse and cart arrived with Mary's family aboard. No sooner were they inside than Jane's family arrived in another cart. This was a huge surprise to the girls, so there were shouts of glee, mixed with excited chatter and embraces.

The girls fetched chairs and began setting the tables and tankards of ale and fine Venetian glasses of Malmsey wine for the guests. Very soon the warm atmosphere and alcohol eased their inhibitions and laughter and good humour naturally followed.

By any standards the luncheon was sumptuous. There was more food on the table than either family would eat in a week. Towards the end, the doctor rose and pointedly avoided toasting the king. He started by toasting the girls and presented Jane and Mary with a jewel box each containing an emerald pendant necklace on a gold chain. Both girls cried with joy as the doctor fastened the necklaces, along with applause from the parents.

The doctor then told the girls to escort their parents on a tour of the house. When they returned both mothers commented on how clean and tidy the house was, and both remarked how envious they were of running water on tap. The girls also told their parents how to use and flush the toilets. The fathers said very little. Their primary concern was that their daughters were being well cared for and that their employment would continue.

Before it got dark, after more ale and wine with cheeses and sliced meats, the carts that John had hired, arrived to take the guests home. The doctor cut the capon in half and insisted that they take the meat home for the following day.

The day must have been a success because both of the girls volunteered for bed warming duties: a novel Christmas present for the doctor.

CHAPTER 13
The clockmaker

Munday 27 January 1662

After Christmass the master doth telle us of his visite to Antwerp where he asketh a jeweller to cleve his large emeralde in 2 partes for presents for his moste favored girls which be me and Mary but the cutter sayeth that the stone be so hye in value that it be a better bargayne to keepeth hole. After barter the master doth gayne 2 emeraldes sette in gold neck chaynes and the difference in silver bullyon.

In London the master doth barter for silkes for us which Mistress Price mayketh wonderous softe nytte shifts which be so quaynte. Mary doth dance in her nytte shift in the eye of the master in a manner that doth show alle her fleshe. Jezabel be her nayme not Mary. The master sayeth we hath fynne countenance beyonde measure and wilt reward a paynter to maketh a lykeness of us both but in goode grayce we sayeth nay as strayngers may see the lykeness.

The master seeketh a fynne clock that doth keepe goode tyme for his bedchaymber and doth meet agayne the clocke mayker and engrayver of grayte skille and moste delicayte who doth promise soon a clock withe the anker pendulum which nowte gayne or luz 1 seconde in a day. Twas he who mayketh the pendulum clock and the calendar in the pharma. The master doth barter a tele scoppe for his boat and maketh inquyrie if the apprentice be willinge to tayketh a shoppe in Wareham.

May the Lord keepeth our dear master sayfe at sea.

Munday 27 January 1662

Jane's next memoir tells us more about the emerald necklaces that the doctor gave the girls at Christmas time. During his trip to Antwerp, the centre of cutting and polishing precious stones at that period, the doctor tried to get his large but crude emerald cut in two as presents for the girls. The jeweller told him that the stone was infinitely more valuable in one piece because it was so large.

We can imagine that they haggled and eventually agreed a price for the huge stone in exchange for two smaller emerald pendants and a cash sum in bullion.

The doctor still had his pouch of assorted smaller stones.

The doctor was still intent on assembling a team of craftsmen. During a trip to London to buy the girls silk for nightdresses he met again the clock-maker who made his pendulum clock and the calendar, looking for a more accurate clock for his house. If the truth be known he was probably searching for a more accurate timepiece to complete his set of standards: mass, length and time.

The doctor judged the workmanship of the apprentice to be excellent and the quality of his engraving was unmatched. The apprentice also professed knowledge of very accurate clocks that could show minutes and seconds, although he had not built such a clock yet. I think we can assume that he was aware of Hooke's anchor escapement and the work of Huygens. It would not have been too difficult to make a simple pendulum with an accurate swing of one second. What was more difficult was to maintain that swing for 24 hours or more consistently.

We don't know for sure, but I would guess that the doctor asked whether the apprentice had a wife and children, and of course about his health. It must have been in his mind to entice the clockmaker away to Wareham to join his team, but he didn't make an offer at that stage. He did, however, purchase an excellent telescope for his boat.

Clockmakers didn't just make clocks, they made delicate and accurate instruments of any kind. They were accustomed to working to very fine tolerances that often required magnifying glasses to see, so they were familiar and skilled with optics and lenses, although lens grinding would have been done by other specialists.

The girls were thrilled with the fine silks that the doctor had purchased at great expense and could not wait for Mrs Price to create luxurious night dresses for them. Jane records that they paraded these dresses in front of the doctor for his approval. It seems that Mary in particular brazenly exposed too much flesh beneath the silk which embarrassed Jane. Clearly John must have been impressed because he told them that he wanted to commission a painter to capture their beauty. The girls were reluctant to agree in case anyone should see the revealing paintings.

It is interesting that Jane never mentions Tyneham House, the big manor hiding in the woods just outside the village. This was the home of the Williams family or at least it belonged to them as well as most of the land. The Williams were landed gentry and had other estates in Dorset. It is likely that some of the villagers were employed at the big house, or most likely farming the land, probably under the supervision of a trusted bailiff. The landed gentry rarely spoke to ordinary folk, unlike the doctor, so Jane would have no knowledge of them apart from gossip, besides, as far as she was concerned she, Mary and the doctor were the new gentry and focus of the village.

Tyneham House and the lands were sold to Nathaniel Bond in 1683 and even he didn't live at the house for long before moving to Creech Grange in 1691.

CHAPTER 14
Sailing

Tewsday 11 February 1662

Me and Mary spayke withe Robert Miller, a fisherman of Worbarrow who oft sayleth with the master in his craffte and he sayeth it be the goodest boat he ever didst sayle, but the master be ever myndfulle to impruffe it by chaynginge the main stays to woode and neuwe ways to reefe the sayles from insyde the cabin. It rydeth welle in hye seas and doth tack welle and tis quicke lyke no other withe a maste of 20 feet and a hye boom. It canst not be tipped even by 4 men. Nere shores it sayleth in moste shallow waters even to Wareham on the river and hath comforts in the cabin which openeth at the roof for 4 personnes and there be hot stones to warme them and at the helm and a yron privie for the ladies. It be sayfe with oars and nowte need of the bilges. Robert sayeth that the master be a fynne navigaytor with the quadrant and doth let the fishermen to fish with nets from the boat of a Friday for alle the village.

Of a fynne day in the month of June in the Year of our Lord 1661 Robert and the master doth sayle by

Hastings withe foode and ale for the nytte and thence into London at Wapping to meet the factor Joseph who doth ryde with them. The boat tayketh abord a clock and brasses and Delft tyles and bowles and glasse wares then on the morrow sayleth by Bryton and after, the wind doth blow in fayvore and the boat cometh apon Brandy Bay so quicke after noone that Robert be much in awe.

May the goode Lord keepeth sayfe men who sayle the seas.

Tewsday 11 February 1662

This memoir tells us something about the doctor's new boat that was built by Mr Salter at his yard in Swanwich (Swanage). The reason Jane wrote this account is probably because the doctor went on and on about his new toy and what an excellent boat it was. She gleaned much of the detail from a local fisherman in Worbarrow.

Her account tells us that the doctor spent a great deal of time learning how to sail his boat in the company of one or more fishermen from Worbarrow during the period 1660-1661. Most of the time they were in sight of land but sometimes, usually on a Friday they cast nets for fish and the whole village feasted on the catch.

It was unusually low in the water and could not be tipped over despite a 20 foot mast, even when 4 fishermen tried. According to Robert Miller (one of the fishermen) it was the easiest and fastest boat he'd ever sailed. Most of all he liked the fact that the binnacle and the helm were inside the boat protected from the weather. The two hulls were so watertight that they rarely used the bilge pumps and they could raise or reef the sail in a trice (quickly). Even at speed it could turn without heeling, although the doctor always slowed before a tack to avoid the prow diving and the stern lifting. Robert also liked the high boom which meant nobody had to fear it hitting their heads.

In Robert's opinion it was an excellent seaworthy craft, he mentioned the doctor wanted to change the forestays with wooden spars, and he wanted to devise a way to reef the sails from the cabin. Jane would not have been familiar with these sailing terms and could have misunderstood them. Nowhere is there any mention that the doctor actually carried out these modifications.

The boat also had two oars (one on each side) which were stowed on the cabin roof. This meant the boat could be manoeuvred very easily when docking. The passenger cabin opened at the top, and inside it could seat four people comfortably. There was even a small iron privy inside too. What amazed Robert were the two 'basket' heaters to keep passengers and the crew warm. Heating on ships or boats was unheard of. Obviously Robert was not aware that the doctor had similar heaters in his house.

Not only was the doctor testing the boat, but also his seafaring skills and ability to navigate with an English quadrant. Periodically they sailed out of sight of land to test whether they could navigate back again. It was just as well that Robert knew the coastline like the back of his hand because the maps of the time were not exactly accurate. Fortunately the draught of the boat (the depth of water to float) was so small that they could even sail over the sand banks and shallows of Poole harbour without running aground. They could also sail up the river Frome to Wareham, which pleased the doctor.

Eventually the doctor and Robert were confident enough to sail the boat to London (approximately 300 miles), which they did in June 1661, taking two days with a stop overnight anchored off the coast of Hastings. They could have gone ashore to find an inn, but the doctor had thoughtfully brought a hamper and ale for the journey. There is no mention of who stood watch during the night.

The following day they moored at Wapping so that John could proudly show his boat to his friend Joseph, who was so impressed that he insisted on taking a ride. Later they took on a clock (and probably the calendar), some Delft china bowls and tiles, brassware and some Venetian glass for the doctor's house. It was late afternoon when they tacked down the Thames before the north-east wind sped them to the coast off Brighton. Despite a brewing storm and heavy seas they spent the night aboard.

At dawn with a following wind they set full sail and ran with the wind as fast as the craft would go. The sky was so grey that the doctor could not use his quadrant and before Robert realised, they arrived in Brandy Bay. It was only mid afternoon when they beached the boat in Worbarrow bay. As a fisherman, Robert would have known all the local landmarks. In particular Portland Bill, which at that time was an island at certain times in the tide, with two distinctive rocks at the tip. However, on this particular day this landmark was not visible.

Brandy Bay is the local name that Jane knew the bay as, regardless of whatever its true name was. Imported wines and spirits were subject to taxes of one sort or another so for at least a century smuggling wines and spirits from France had been endemic all along the south coast of England: a practice that continued for at least two more centuries. It is quite possible that the fishermen of Worbarrow periodically used the doctor's boat for this purpose to suppliment their meagre earnings.

CHAPTER 15
A Broken Leg

Wensday 19 March 1662

A week ago Edwin cometh layte in dire distress and doth telle to Mary to bringeth the master unto Steeple for a boy hast falle from the roofe. The master doth command me to ryde withe him whylst Mary wilt staye withe Edwin to care for the house and animals.

The master dothe look at the boy to assay his infirms and doth see cleare that the boy hast broke a bone in the legge which alle couldst see so he doth carrie the boy to his bed and giveth the boy a potion to ease the payne. The master then asketh for my emeralde which methinks be moste straynge and dothe hold it in the sun to glister and commandeth (the) boy to sette his gayze apon the jewel and see nowte else. He telleth the boy to feel sleepie agayne and agayne and lo the boy doth falle asleep. The master telleth the boy to feel no payne in the broke legge and to feel happie and I do swear the boy ddidst smyle in his sleepe. I never didst see suche before.

Now the master doth pull the broke legge and doth putte the bone back and asketh the madame for boiled water to cleaneth the wound and after he doth wash it withe brandie and alom to stoppe the bloode. MJ doth then cute a hair from the tayle of his horse and doth boil it in water and then brandie and commandeth me to stitch the fleshe together with a needle and the haire from the horse. After, he putteth honie on the wound and doth bynde it withe cleene linen and woode stickes to stoppeth the bones to move. Alle the while the boy doth feel nowte and dist not once cry out.

The worde of this miracle doth travel from villayge to villayge lyke fyre that the master doth tayketh awaye payne withe a magic green jewel. The master sayeth to me that it be not magic but a verie firme beleiffe that the payne be not there. He doth confess that the potion of laudnum also helpeth muche.

The next day Ruttyand the master didst attended the boy to mayketh better stickes with straps of lether to stoppeth the bonoe to mov and Rutty mayketh 2 woode stickes which fit under the arms so that the boy canst walk.

It be of grayte import to the master but I know not why, to verify the matters of length, wayte and capacitie of *divers matters. The master goeth even unto London to copie a cloth yard on a brass sticke and to copie a pound wayte. The doctor sayeth a gallon be nowte sense, the gallon be a measure of a square pot 7 inch long and 4 inch wyde and 8 inch deepe and be the sayme for all matter and full withe 8 pynts. I knoweth my numbers fulle welle and do fynde his inquyrie a mysterie which I putte here in goode faythe that the master hath reason. Joseph doth telle the master that insyde the barrels of powder from Ragussa there be wax canvas sacks and at Wapping he doth keep the powder in salt glayzed jars which be made at Woolwich to keepeth the powder stronge.*

May the goode Lord keepeth the master sayfe.

Wensday 19 March 1662

The next memoir begins with a detailed account of the doctor doing his job as a doctor. It appears that Edwin arrived late one day and through Mary pleaded for the doctor to attend a boy who had fallen from the roof in the village of Steeple.

The doctor commanded Jane to be his assistant and they rode off together to see what could be done. It seems the boy had broken his leg and the bone end was visible through a gash in his flesh. No doubt it was bleeding badly.

The doctor immediately gave the boy a potion of laudnum (morphine) to kill the pain and firmly commanded the boy to be silent. From Jane's account it would appear that the doctor was attempting to use hypnosis, aided by the morphine, although she obviously doesn't use the word hypnosis. It also appears to have been successful, much to Jane's surprise. The doctor reset the bone by feel and then washed the wound with boiled water, alcohol and finally alum to stop the bleeding. After that the doctor instructed Jane to stitch the wound with horse hair (sterilized) and then sealed the wound with honey before binding it with linen and wooden splints.

The following day the doctor, in the company of Rutty the carpenter, attended the boy again and made better splints with leather straps, and a pair of crutches. No doubt the doctor also checked for signs of infection although Jane doesn't say so. We learn from a later memoir that the boy recovered fully.

In the circumstances I think he doctor did exceedingly well despite the lack of medication and equipment. Jane describes the event as miraculous, and in particular the 'trick' with the sparkling emerald to induce a hypnotic state. Clearly people of the time would have considered this to be magic, but in reality it is likely that the doctor knew of such practices in the orient (Japan and China) as a result of the trade monopoly that existed between Holland and Japan. I suspect this was the first time that the doctor had tried this technique and to be on the safe side he also administered morphine; probably a heavy dose.

The doctor confessed to Jane that it definitely was not magic but more a case of the willingness of the patient to absolutely and firmly believe in the ability of the doctor to take the pain away: a matter of faith. Whatever the real reason, the legend that passed from village to village was that it was magic or a miracle.

This was dangerous territory because practicing witchcraft was punishable by torture and death. It is unlikely that a gentleman would be accused of witchcraft but it could happen, and this was the last thing that the doctor would want. Earlier that century hundreds of people had been put to death for witchcraft for using magic to do the devil's work. The doctor knew only too well that logic was no defence against superstition. Fortunately the doctor had a good reputation for kindness and good deeds, so it is unlikely that he would have been accused.

The antiseptic 'brandie' that Jane refers to was almost certainly not real French Brandy, which would have been far too expensive, but more likely very strong medicinal alcohol (ethanol) that was widely used by Apothecaries for making tinctures, such as tincture of laudnum. Most likely, the alcohol would have been a constant boiling point mixture of about 68% alcohol in water, which makes it about twice the strength of modern spirits such as whisky, rum, gin or vodka. With no flavouring and undiluted, this alcohol would have been virtually undrinkable. In this form the alcohol would have been a very effective sterilizing agent.

I am sure that the rest of the memoir was of very little interest to Jane, but I suspect she wrote it to demonstrate the doctor's determination, dedication and possibly obsession once he got an idea into his head, even if she thought the problem was insignificant or not worth bothering with. It also reveals her growing confidence because she even questions why the doctor is so concerned with weights and measures.

She was completely familiar with the basic coinage of the day: twelve pennies make a silver shilling, and twenty silver shillings make a pound. In the alphabet exercise Jane writes the numbers 1 to 12 because that is how she would have learnt to count since the monetary system was duodecimal at that time and continued until 1972. Originally 20 shillings did weigh one pound weight of silver but by the 17th century 20 shillings were worth less than a pound weight of silver. Coin cutting was also widely practiced to produce coins of less value than a penny, such as the half penny and the quarter penny (farthing). Intermediate coins of penny multiples were also in circulation such as the tuppence (two pence), the threpence (three pence) and the groat (four pence) and the sixpence. It is likely that Jane might have known that there were several other coins of greater value than the shilling in circulation such as the half crown (two sillings and six pence), the crown (five shillings) and the gold double crown (ten shillings), but it is doubtful that she would have ever seen coins of this value.

She also knew, because she had been taught that 12 inches make a foot, and 3 feet make a yard. She knew about area measures such as acres and other land measures such as miles, furlongs, rods and poles. It is doubtful if she knew that five and half feet make a rod. Even nowadays school kids do not always make a connection between length and distance. In the UK length and distance are still measured in completely different units (metric for length and miles for distance).

Jane was no doubt familiar with certain basic measures of weight: 16 ounces make one pound, 14 pounds make a stone, 8 stones make a hundredweight, and possibly she knew that 20 hundredweights make a ton. Again in the UK schools teach the metric system (Kgm) but if ask most people how much they weigh they will tell you in stones and pounds while in the US everybody will tell you in pounds.

She would not have been familiar with the concept of volume, but she certainly knew that 4 gills make a pint and 8 pints make a gallon. There were many other units for measuring liquid volumes but she would have no use for them. Likewise there was a system for measuring the volumes of dry goods such as bushels, but again she would have no use for it in her everyday life.

It is all very well knowing these quantities by rote, but she, like most people, had no idea how these units were defined. As far as she was concerned she bought cloth by the yard as measured with a wooden or brass rule. She bought ale as measured by a pint beer pot or mug. She bought fish or meat by the pound as measured by an iron weight on the scales.

The doctor, on the other hand did understand about standards. If he prescribed medicine by weight, then he had to be sure the Apothecary was using exactly the same measure to dispense that weight. Guesswork could be fatal.

Industry was not yet at the stage where components were made in different places and when they came together they had to fit. The house builder and the carpenter didn't build the house and windows separately and hope that they would fit: the builder made the window opening and then the carpenter made a window to fit the hole. Trial and error was endemic, but it had no place in the doctor's world: he couldn't draw trial and error on paper.

The doctor had been fortunate in Ragussa. He had personally defined his own standard weight of silver (50 shillings) that was equivalent to a standard volume of powder (a barrel). He would have preferred to use nationally recognized standards, so he set about obtaining copies of those standards, which entailed a visit to London.

John argued quite correctly that the current volume measures (gallons and pints) were quite arbitrary because they depended on the substance being measured. He was in favour of a volume defined by dimensions such as the cubic foot or cubic inch. Consequently, in a similar arbitrary way he defined the

Leiden gallon (independent of liquid) as 224 cubic inches and a pint was 28 cubic inches and a gill was 7 cubic inches (a gill short of a standard wine gallon - 231 cubic inches).

Jane mentions that Joseph now uses waxed sacks inside the barrels of Dalmatian insecticide powder and transfers the powder to salt glazed jars, made by a pottery at Woolwich, in his warehouse in Wapping in order to preserve the potency of the powder. She doesn't tells us what size the jars are, but I think we can assume the the doctor knew, and that he was well aware of the cubic capacity of the barrels. The fact that this information comes from Joseph suggests that he now organizes the annual collection of the powder from Ragussa and that he is importing as much powder as the doctor.

On his visit to London the doctor discovered that a standard cloth yard existed at the Merchant Taylors Hall in Threadneedle street which he visited to see the brass standard and to make a copy by marking a brass rod of his own.

John probably discovered that the Exchequer kept a brass copy of an Elizabethan standard pound weight but he probably could not get access to this object so he would have chosen the simple alternative of going to a reputable clock and instrument maker and purchasing a double pan balance with a certified collection of weights from one pound down to one ounce. He almost certainly had a similar balance that measured in grains for weighing medicines.

John could have decided to create his own standards from scratch but he was a pragmatist, not a revolutionary or an evangelist. He just wanted a framework within which he could work and share with others on common ground.

Despite its complexity the English (or Imperial) system of weights and measures was exported across the globe and persisted for several centuries and in part still lingers on in the US and in the UK despite attempts by the EU to eradicate it over the past 40 years.

From this point onwards the memoirs become increasingly technical: far beyond Jane's comprehension. In effect the memoirs are not about Jane at all, they are about her employer. In her eyes her own life was not worth writing about. What mattered was what the doctor was thinking and doing. As a result she often wrote about concepts, ideas and devices about which she knew nothing. They were beyond her understanding and for the most part beyond her interest. She writes her memoirs as more of a duty to record the obscure and mysterious activities of the doctor.

In a way we should be grateful that she did because her faithful records contain unwitting but valuable detailed information. The doctor himself, unlike his contemporaries, was more concerned with practical achievement rather than recording the details for posterity. Perhaps he intended to do this later in life. There is almost an element of desperation in the way in which the doctor wants to realize his ideas in practice rather than spend time documenting them. He is clearly out-of-step with the times. He would have been more at home in the present day where we would expect results in a month and not have to wait years.

CHAPTER 16
Swimming

Munday 6 July 1663

Summer this year hath been hot for mennie months but the house be pleasant cool. The master tayketh us to the sands to cool in the sea. At first we be moste modest in our naykedness but we art begyled by the cool water. The master doth shew us the manner to swimme which we doth both enjoy. Out from the sea MJ doth cover and dry us withe blankettes. Agayne we doth visite the sands mennie times and hath a screene of blankettes on sticks which doth save us from the wind and from the eye of strangers.

In tyme the master sayeth that we be goode swimmers and tayketh us aborde his boat to swimme in deepe water and laye in the sun beyonde the eyes of strayngers. The master hath sweet smellinge oils and creemes that mayketh the skinne soft which he doth rub withe gentle hands on alle our bodie parts which now be now gold and browne as dung.

By day we doth oft dress in nytte shifts to keepeth cool. Mary asketh Mistress Price to mayketh us short breeches in linen so we hath nowte neede of petticotes on the sands. Mary doth complayn the breeches hath no comfort so Mistress Price doth cutte them short but doth not show our modestie.

In the layte evenings the master doth tutor us withe straynge melodies and rithms on the tayble top from his trybe in the Neuwe Worlde which doth mayke Mary dance and twerle in odd ways. The master doth promiss a harpsichord for us to play these mistick melodies.

One hot day the master tayketh us to swimme in the sea and thence to Wareham in the boat to cleene the cottage next the carpenter for the familie of William Parsons, the clocke mayker which doth please the master. Rutty doth mayke a bed and cotte and tayble for the familie and the chylde.

Prayse be to the Lord for the goode summer and a goode harvest.

Munday 6 July 1663

According to Jane's account the summer of 1663 was hot, although the house remained beautifully cool at night (it was well insulated). In the daytime when nobody was about on the beach at Worbarrow, the doctor taught them how to swim. They swam naked which embarrassed the girls at first, but once in the water they were safe from preying eyes. Out of the water they covered themselves with woollen blankets to preserve their modesty.

A few days later they went to the beach again, but this time the doctor made a wind shield from blankets nailed to wooden sticks that were stuck in the sand. It protected them from the breeze and protected their modesty, so that they could lie in the sun. The doctor even made creams and oils so they would not burn in the sun. It is likely that the girls had never sunbathed before and would be unaware of its affect on their skin.

The trio repeated these visits almost daily until the doctor was convinced that they could swim proficiently. Jane records that Mary and the doctor turned brown in the sun whereas she turned golden (Mary and the doctor were probably dark haired, whereas Jane was blond). The doctor then began taking them out to sea in the boat to swim and sunbathe without fears of being seen naked. By the end of summer the girls were good swimmers and all were as brown as 'dung'.

The girls had taken to wearing their new silk night shifts around the house even though the slightest breeze revealed all. At Mary's instigation, Mrs Price made the girls a pair of short linen breeches. Again at Mary's instigation these breeches were shortened even more so that they only just concealed their modesty. The girls were now happy enough to walk through the village in shifts and top skirts, and throw off their top skirts on the beach.

In the long light evenings they drank wine and the doctor taught them strange melodies and dances while they beat compelling rhythms with their hands on the kitchen table. Often Mary danced to the melodies but some were slow and melancholy. The doctor said that they were tribal songs and dances from the New World. The doctor promised to buy a harpsichord so that the girls could play these songs for him.

We know that John must have done a deal with the apprentice clockmaker, because Jane tells us that they took the boat to Wareham and swept out the empty cottage next to the carpenter and the blacksmith. They also put furniture made by 'Rutty', the carpenter, into the house, including a bed and a cot. The doctor told them that William Parsons, the clockmaker from London, and his family were renting the house in a few days. This was the same clock-maker who made the pendulum clock and the calendar and had so impressed the doctor with his skills and engraving.

CHAPTER 17
Roads

Sunday 11 October 1663

The boy from Steeple withe the broke legge cometh this day and giveth thanks to the master and showeth how goode it be mended. Mary and me doth gossip withe alle fowlkes twixt Tyneham and Wareham on the goodest deedes of the master and his repute for a generous kyndlie nature and his goode words for alle folkes as equals. In church today after prayer he spake to alle sayinge the road to Wareham be so poor and needeth to be mayde goode by efforte of the villayge in the stout manner of roades payved by Romans so it be smoothe for man or cart in benefit for alle. He doth implore the fowlkes to maketh it come to pass by example to divers other villayges on the waye to do the sayme to Wareham. A dozen hands doth show to agree and werke begineth nere to Egliston.

The Roman manner be a trench 8 feete wyde of stone shardes under clay and gritte rolled harde by a barrel of water and thence paved in blockes of stone cobbles layde prowde not flatte for the rayne to drayne. The master sayeth that a myle canst be mayde by 3 months.

May the goode Lord be with alle who mayketh the roade to Wareham.

Sunday 11 October 1663

In this day and age we take roads for granted, but in the mid 17th century the roads in England were a mess. Almost two thousand years earlier the Romans realised the importance of road communication for moving armies, goods and materials around a conquered country, so one of their top priorities was to develop an infra structure of good roads. Many routes of the roads that were built with slave labour across England to connect the major cities of the time still exist to this day.

After the Romans left, the Britons who were left behind had neither the will nor the technology to maintain or extend this network, and so it fell into decline. The Roman network only connected the major population centres: small towns and villages depended on tracks beaten by the feet of time. By the 17th century there was little to tell the roads and local tracks apart.

Stagecoach travel was in its infancy as were well-surfaced toll roads. Typically, a simple 150-mile journey from Bristol to London could take five days or even more in bad weather. Outside London, little wonder that long journeys were undertaken by sea and overland journeys were rarely in excess of five to ten miles or so: the distance between villages or the nearest market town. With no postal service, except for King's Messengers (on horseback), rural England was essentially isolated.

The doctor was obviously well aware of the limitations of travel at the time from his personal experiences. He made almost daily visits to Wareham (about five miles on horseback), and periodic visits by his boat to his friend, Joseph Vanderhoek, and other business associates in London. We know that the good doctor was not just a physician: he was a polymath like many of his contemporaries such as Newton, Boyle, and Hooke. This was the beginning of the 'age of enlightenment' and John was keenly aware of what the future might promise. He was also aware that the future he anticipated would not just happen on it's own.

Experience had already taught him that his pragmatic approach and leadership could make things happen. He was fully aware that he couldn't do much on his own, but under his direction and leadership he had built a kattumaram (catamaran) to make long distance travel easier, and a clean and hygienic house, and a lucrative business based on insecticide derived from the Dalmatian daisy.

There was also a determined, obsessive side to his personality, which is clearly evident in his attitudes and beliefs about personal cleanliness, even though they were out of step with the times. He was a highly motivated, 'driven' man, with unshakable confidence in his own abilities. He was quite happy, like Paracelsus, to set aside as complete rubbish, some of the current medical practices and remedies. His enquiring mind wanted practical proof of everything: a growing feature of all the scientific discoveries of the time.

Such a man wouldn't let poor roads stand in his way. The most well trodden path was the route to Wareham, as this was the nearest market town. His sermon to the villagers after prayers one Sunday in October 1663 demonstrates his attempt to engage them into making this a real road. He already had a reputation, far and wide, for his kindness and generosity and he doubtless knew that he could capture their attention and support, as Jane's description of the event clearly shows. He also had a reputation for miraculous powers since the young boy from Steeple had so fully recovered from his broken leg. Self-interest would be the principal driving force for the village to do their part. Once they had completed the road from Tyneham to the next village, it would be a working example for all the other villages along the route to follow suit. The villagers were not expected to pave the whole road to Wareham on their own and they were not expected to complete the task over-night.

Jane's account also shows that the doctor knew that he didn't have the resources to match the way that Roman roads were built (I estimate that he would need about 2000 cubic feet of lime mortar 'concrete' for every mile of road built). The limestone was freely available in countless nearby quarries, but there were just not enough trees to burn to convert this to lime mortar. The good doctor, in his usual pragmatic way, solved this problem by substituting local clay instead of mortar. Like limestone, there was an abundant free local source, but from a technical point of view clay was not as durable as concrete. Clay expands when wet and shrinks when dry. Frequent rain would have kept the clay moist and stable, so he was gambling that any rare, long hot dry spells of weather would not dry out the clay enough to cause cracks big enough for the large road surface rocks to fall into.

Her account suggests that the doctor estimated a mile of road, eight feet wide (the standard Roman width), would take the volunteers nearly three months to build. The weather would probably restrict building work to just six months in the year. If the other villages joined in the task, then the road to Wareham could be completed in two to four years. It has to be remembered that in those days 'time' was not as urgent as it is nowadays, so such a timetable would not have been so daunting for the villagers. They were accustomed to patience.

Jane does not give us much detail about how the road was constructed, but we can make some educated guesses about this issue. It would have made sense to start the road at the nearest quarry at Egliston, simply because the horse and cart carrying the stones would find it easier to travel along a well made surface to reach the current point where the stones were needed. We know that John would be using Roman road construction as a model, so in all probability the road foundations would have been about a foot deep, consisting of six inches of crushed stone with six inches of a stiff dough-like mixture of clay, sand and gravel, topped with limestone sets (roughly square cobbles) laid with a crown in the centre to provide quick drainage. The thick cobbles, grouted with soft clay, would provide the hard working surface. The spoil from the foundations would have been dumped either side. Over time, weeds and grass would consolidate the spoil heaps into drainage ditches.

The account does mention the use of a water filled barrel as a roller to tamp down and compress the foundation layers, but doesn't say what size this barrel was. To be effective, the water barrel would need to be at least a half to one ton in weight. Although the account does not mention who surveyed the route, it is most likely that John did this himself, and set out wooden pegs or sticks to mark the course and width of the road. Again, the account tells us that the villagers assembled every Saturday, except harvest time and bad weather, and that the team of volunteers numbered 'a dozen'. There is no indication whether this dozen included people at the quarry, the clay pits, or at the beach collecting sand and gravel. Whatever the number of volunteers, it was a very high proportion of the village population.

You might ask, why would so many people offer to work so hard for nothing? Firstly, there was a rigid class system in operation that was designed to ensure that everybody 'knew their place' in society and that they accepted the situation with stoic resignation. Any dissent was brutally crushed. Basically the working poor did what they were told to do. The upper classes truly believed that they were somehow 'better' than the lower classes so they were entitled to be in charge to do the telling. The King even believed, that he was ordained by God to occupy that position. This was pushing the limits of credibility too far, so the government of the day beheaded the King in 1649.

Not surprisingly the ordinary working people were resentful and suspicious of the gentry and upper classes. Unfortunately Doctor Leiden would have been considered gentry by virtue of his occupation, but in his case he didn't act like gentry. He would speak to ordinary folk as equals, and he was generous, kind and considerate. He also offered the poor his services as a doctor for free, and only charged the rich. This set the doctor apart from his class. He still received the inbred deference from the lower classes, but it was given out of respect. They helped him because he helped them.

The local landowners may well have been the idle rich, but they were not stupid. They could see that an improved network of roads in the countryside would benefit them far more than it would ever benefit the poor devils that were building the roads. Firstly the value of their lands would increase as a result of better transport. Trade across the countryside would increase. Most of the landowners also had other local business interests so better transportation of goods had to be in their best interests. There is little doubt that the doctor would have been given huge encouragement from his own class in support of such a noble venture.

CHAPTER 18
Oil lamps

Tewsday 29 March 1664

Winter hast been moste cruel this year but Christ Mass wast well spent withe our families in the house of the master and it be warme with fyres and baskettes of hot stones alle abouts, even in the cowshed and the stayble in boxes fulle with pumice. MJ giveth to us a Ruckers harpsichord which doth sound sweete and divers silke breeches which afore our families maketh us to blushe.

Without fore warninge Jake and Rutty and Will doth mayketh a smalle walnut cabinette that contayne a fynne tooth combe with our naymes on the brass handle. These be proper gentlemen and the master be so prowde. By morninge each day we doth cleene alle candlesticks which be a grayte messe and we doth complayne to the master for oil lamps. The soute dishes be nowte messe for we hath a stone jar withe turpentine and a moppe and woode grippes. Mary doth telle that oil be mayde at Kimmeridge nere here.

The master doth ryde forth to Kimmeridge which stinke and see the beach afyre with flaymes and smoke and blackstone alle aboutes, which some personnes do carve as jewels but MJ doth barter the blackstone alone and some stinkinge yellow oil which he witness doth burn bryte withe smoke.

The master be myndefulle to purifie the oil in a lyke manner to talle stills he hath seen in Hollande. Forthwithe Jake and MJ mayketh a talle stille 1 yard hye and half a foote across with blackstone at the bottom and a baskette of pumice above and a spoute at the top. There be no leekes so Jake bringeth charcoals from the forge and sette them about the stille. In tyme when the stille hot as solder the spoute doth drippe cleare droppes which gather in a stone jar tille no more be seen. The oil be more cleare and doth burn a rope bryte and not so stinkinge. In the stille there be left a yellow pitche which MJ sayeth maybe agin water and goode for the neuwe rode. In Wareham be there nowte lampes to barter so MJ doth sayle to London.

The plague be amocke in Amsterdam and alle shippes of Hollande be in quanratine for 30 days which mayketh the factor sore vexed and rumore hast 40 days in the coffee shoppe amidst uprore.

The master sayeth unto Joseph be myndefulle of his prophesie and gather up thyne familie and thy servants if the plague doth come and tayketh refuge in thy house withe foode and water and the dustinge pwder tille the plague be done.

In muche haste the master doth barter oil lamps and oil and a pot of dustinge powder and doth flee London as quicke as the winde. The master confyde that if the plague be here in Tyneham we wilt staye in the house a fulle year if needes be. He also telleth Mary and me that he didst attende a companie of lawyers to maketh a testament that we both shalt both inherit his propertie and fortune if he be strucke downe withe the playgue. We both doth crie with miserie for it be the love of the master that we want and not his fortune.

Mary doth falle sick with fever and aykinge bones on a Sunday after the master doth return from London. I be frit lest it be the plague, but MJ be certayne tis not plague for it be soon after his visite to London and she hath no swellinge. Mary doth telle that her Sire hath a bad coffe with grayte fatigue and the master sayeth Mary hath the same maladie so she asketh for the

166

magic emeralde sleepe and the master doth that the magic sleepe owlie tayketh awaye payne and canst not tayketh the illness. The master commandeth me to sew 3 masks of linen like our bleeding pads and fulle withe woole to cover the mouth and nose which we must ware in the room of Mary lest we also suffer the maladie.MJ then mayketh a pottage with mennie herbes and a potion of tinkture of laudnum with honie and mint which doth mayke her sleepe with no coffe. The master commandeth that we wash hands after we be in the room of Mary and wype our hands with brandie afore we tuche others. I cutteth mennie linen kercheffes Mary to wype her nose and after they be soiled the master putteth them to fyrer.

Mary asketh to suckle his manhood for tis a common beleefe that man seed doth cure mennie ills and maladies. The master sayeth tis nonsense but Mary pleadeth more. Methinks that if this be true then canst I not have the sayme cure. The master agayne proteste that it be nonsense but his seed doth work for both. Mary doth recover in 4 days but the coffe didst last tille month end and I didst never suffer the maladie.

Prayse be unto the Lord that the maladie be not the plague for Mary be as a sister.

Tewsday 29 March 1664

Historical records tell us that the winter of 1663/64 was particularly harsh. Despite this, the house insulation and wire baskets containing hot stones kept the house warm for the Christmas festivities with the family. The doctor even put a basket heater, in a box full of pumice, in the cowshed and the stable because it was so cold.

The girls were presented with a Ruckers harpsichord (imported by John from Antwerp) as the doctor had promised, as well as several pairs of silk breeches made by Mrs Price, which made the girls blush in front of their parents. Mary tried to pick out a tune on the keyboard to impress her parents and the doctor.

The girls also had a present from the blacksmith, carpenter and the clockmaker. They had collaborated to make walnut presentation boxes each containing a fine toothed comb of steel needles with their names engraved on the polished brass handle. This was a complete surprise to the doctor who inspected the craftsmanship with admiration. Even without the doctor, his team were thinking for themselves collectively. No doubt John could see a lucrative market for these combs, selling on the back of his trade in insecticide.

Some time later the girls complained about how wasteful and messy candles are. The doctor already knew how many candles they were burning every week because he had to pay for them, so he promised to look into replacing them with oil lamps. It got dark so early at this time of year that they were using many more candles than normal. It was Mary who said there was rumour that lamp oil was being made at Kimmeridge, only a few miles away.

John took a ride to Kimmeridge (the present site of the oldest on-land oil well in England at Wytch Farm) to verify the rumour, which proved to be correct. The village itself had a strange smell that he traced to the beach. Some villagers were collecting 'blackstone' (oil shale) from the beach and heating it in iron kettles to make an evil smelling yellowish liquid, which they called lamp oil. They lit a lamp to show the doctor how good it was. It certainly burnt with a bright yellow flame, but it was very smoky and had a bad smell too.

Other villagers tried to sell him ornaments carved in the 'blackstone' (simulated Jet). Instead, John bought a sack full of the raw 'blackstone'. There were several fires on the beach where the villagers were using the 'blackstone' as fuel to heat the kettles, but there were also unattended fires too. The beach was a barren land of smoke and smouldering flames.

On the way back to Wareham it occurred to John that the lamp oil made from 'blackstone' could be purified to reduce the smell and the soot. He had seen 'column' stills for purifying strong alcohol spirits working in Holland and probably assumed a similar method might work with the lamp oil.

At his request Jake built a tall still, 6 inches in diameter and 36 inches tall. The upper part was filled with nuggets of pumice in a wire basket. The lower part was filled with 'blackstones'. John knew that the lamp oil was dangerous and could be ignited very easily but he could see no leaks, so Jake fetched charcoal from the forge and with the aid of bellows they soon had a blaze around the still bottom. After a time drops of clear liquid at the top spout dripped into a stoneware jar just below. Jake used some soft solder to see how hot the metal was (soft solder melts at 180-190 degrees). When there were no more drops, they put out the fire and took out the basket of pumice. In the bottom was dark yellowish evil smelling liquid that solidified when it cooled.

Jake dipped some rope into the refined lamp oil and it burnt with virtually no smell and with much less smoke. John told Jake that if the foul smelling pitch at the bottom was waterproof he would use it on the road being built to Wareham to protect the foundations.

Wareham was not yet wealthy enough to stock oil lamps: it was a candle powered economy. This meant a trip to London for John.

Joseph was distraught because several of his ships had been quarantined for 30 days because they were from a city infected with plague (Amsterdam). At a nearby coffee shop, the place was buzzing with news that the quarantine might soon be increased to 40 days. There were also rumours that the plague had already arrived.

John reminded Joseph of his prediction of the coming epidemic and urged him to take refuge in his house with his servants if the death rate begins to rise sharply. They should use the Dalmatian powder frequently and stock up with food, and should not have contact closer than ten feet with anyone.

John had come to buy oil lamps and oil, which he did. He also collected a pot of Dalmation powder and then he and Robert sailed away as quickly as possible. His worst nightmare was coming true.

Tyneham was a long way from the city and there was good chance it would be spared. There was no doubt in his mind that he and the girls would survive even if they had to stay in the house for a whole year.

However, the prudent doctor had visited a firm of lawyers in London to make a will in the event of his untimely death. It is a measure of the doctor's love and affection that he named both girls as his heirs to inherit his property and fortune. Jane and Mary both found this provision for the possible death of the doctor very upsetting. No doubt they were pleased that the doctor had secured their future, but the thought of life without the doctor was clearly unimaginable.

Shortly after th doctor returned from London, Mary fell sick with a fever, great fatigue and aching bones. The doctor was certain that this was not the plague because it was too soon after his return from London and she she had no swellings, a characteristic of bubonic plague. Jane was obviously relieved that her 'sister' would not be a victim of the plague. Mary admitted that the previous day she had visited her parents, as she was required to do each week, and that her father had a bad cough. It is most likely that Mary had been infected with influenza although it was not known by that name at the time.

The doctor immediately instructed Jane to make face masks in linen like the menstrual pads the girls wore. She and the doctor wore these masks and wool nose plugs every time they entered Mary's room, and rinsed their hands in brandy and showered afterwards. The doctor also prescribed laudnum (morphine) sweetened with honey and mint (tincture of laudnum is very bitter on its own) to help her sleep and to reduce the inevitable cough that would follow. Even by today's standards of hygiene these were all sensible precautions, however, Mary also believed the common folklore that male semen was the best cure for her ailment. Despite the doctor's disapproval Mary insisted, and so did Jane. They were both more than convinced that oral sex was effective because Jane never caught the 'flu and Mary recoved after four days. The folklore probably originated from incidents such as this, and would be reinforced by such incidents too.

In Mary's case the use of morphine probably accelerated her recovery and certainly relieved her cough, although she would have survived without the morphine or the semen. The girls were extremely fit and healthy individuals with a healthy diet and lifestyle, so it is unlikely that either would have died from contracting a virus such as influenza.

We also have to remember that dread of the plague was endemic and that people would try any remedy regardless of how bizarre it might appear. It is a cedit to the doctor that he diagnosed Mary's illness correctly, much to the relief of all three.

CHAPTER 19
The Great Plague

Thursday 12 October 1665

Agayne the goode Lord doth bless us with a goode summer and harvest. I be gold of skinne and Mary be brown from much swimminge and layinge under the sun. Tyneham be far from London and we know not of the pestilense save gossipe tille it cometh to Wareham with a familie in quarantine.

The master doth ryde with alle haste to the aldermen and sayeth he be a phisicker of Hollande and wilt command the quarantine. By an open window he telleth the personnes insyde to stay wythin and not to tuche others by 10 feete. Foode and water wilt be given by day on a tayble without. Clothes of dead personnes must be putte to fyre. The master giveth dustinge powder to the house and to each house asyde and sayeth the powder wilt halte the spreade of the playgue but cure nowte. The master giveth powder to Jake, Rutty and William. Alle dead bodies must be buried in the instante and not be tuched. By such no others in (Wareham) wilt die.

At Tyneham the master doth disrobe and his clothes to fyre and doth stand nayked for alle to see which maketh us laffe. After MJ hath dusted in the pluvia, still nayked in jest he doth chayse us and sayeth our buttocks wilt feel his hand for our laffinge at him.

Rutty sayeth unto the master that he hath little werke, so the master doth engage him to maketh neuwe windows withe glass and neuwe doors for the house of my Sire and for the Sire of Mary as a giffte afore Christ Mass and the cold winds cometh.

We be of such good cheere that we doth warm the master both and thence so wearie that I sleepeth atop the master alle nytte for he hath nowte strength to move. Mary doth snorte in the nose the nytte long.

The Lord have mercie on those that suffer the plague.

Thursday 12 October 1665

There is a long gap between this memoir and the previous one. Jane offers no reason for this. Perhaps there is a missing memoir, although there is no gap in her continuous record. Probably the doctor was paranoid about the Plague so he didn't travel to London, and quite possibly didn't want the families of the girls to visit at Christmas either, since there was a case of the plague in Wareham. Her frequency of writing had already slowed down, so perhaps she was just fed up with keeping her memoirs up to date.

In London the Bills of Mortality continued to increase in the first months of 1665 and by April 'house quarantine' was introduced. In May the hot weather accelerated the death toll, which reached a peak in a very hot July, killing at least 7000 souls a week. Trade in the city virtually died too as the wealthy attempted to escape the city. So many were dying that their bodies remained rotting in the streets as the doctor predicted. Mass graves were eventually organised and towards winter the death rate slowed and by February 1666 it was just a trickle, and what was left of the population returned to normal. The government sat again in September 1666.

Back in Tyneham the doctor and the girls enjoyed the wonderful summer blissfully unaware of the tragedy unfolding in London.

The first hint of the epidemic occurred in the September when a family in Wareham were quarantined. As soon as the news reached the doctor he raced to Wareham and advised the aldermen what precautions should be taken. John spoke to the distraught family from outside through an open window. He assured them that food and water would left each day on a table outside, otherwise they would have been left to starve. The family must not stand closer than ten feet to other people or to infected people. They must use the dusting powder on themselves and throughout the house everyday. He also told the aldermen to give pouches of dusting powder to the houses on either side of the infected house. Any clothes or fabrics from the infected house must be burnt and not touched. The aldermen were only too pleased that somebody was taking control of this frightening situation.

The doctor warned that any other infections must be quarantined in exactly the same way. Isolation was the only way to halt the plague. He was a physician and he was telling them that there was no cure. The best that they could do was take precautions such as the dusting powder. He emphasised that the powder was not a cure: it would only prevent the plague spreading. Any dead bodies must be buried immediately and must not be touched.

Normally the doctor was easy going and far from being assertive, yet in an emergency he rose to the occasion and moved up a gear to become authorative, issuing commands rather than instructions. He did it when Mary fell sick, and he does it again here in Wareham. His status as a doctor would have helped, but even so he must also have had a commanding presence and considerable self confidence.

Immediately afterwards he went to see Jake, Rutty and William to give them a supply of dusting pouches. When the doctor arrived home he disrobed in the garden and burnt his clothes while the girls watched and laughed. He dusted and showered, then chased the girls around the house threatening to smack their buttocks for laughing at him. Jane observes that she knew he spoke in jest.

There is no mention of the doctor checking his theory about vermin being the carriers of the plague. I suppose he thought that even if he obtained a sample flea or louse from the garments of an infected person, there was no guarantee that the sample vermin were actually infected themselves. He would have to take hundreds of samples to be certain. Taking one sample was risky, and taking hundreds would have been suicide.

This is the second instance that Jane mentions the doctor practicing his profession. I suspect that the good doctor had many visitors to his 'pharma' at the house because he offered his services free to the poor and needy. However, these visits would have been confidential, which is why Jane never mentions them. The doctor would have been the equivalent of a modern day General Practitioner but not a surgeon, although his training at Leiden almost certainly included surgery.

Rutty, the carpenter, was the poor man of the trio of craftsmen and obviously wasn't making enough money like the other two, so he appealed to the doctor for work. As an early Christmas present, the Doctor commissioned Rutty to make new doors and windows with glass for the families of the two girls, before the winter set in. The girls were so grateful that they both 'warmed' the master that night. According to Jane it was so exhausting that she fell asleep on top of the doctor and she notes that Mary snored.

CHAPTER 20
The Fire of London

Sunday 21 October 1666

In the month the neuwe rode to Wareham wast finished and bringeth much cheer to alle. With Edwin in the saddle we taketh our neuwe carrayge so quicke to Wareham in the hour. The carrayge be a fynne neuwe cart with yron springs and 2 large wheeles bedecked in yellow. My Sire mayketh the saddle and harness.

Mary doth spend much tyme at the harpsichord for favore of the master and I be at werke in the garden withe flowers and herbes for the master doth much admyre the smelle.

The master be of grayte concerne and doth worrie withe neuwes of Joseph and his familie and curious to know that he survyve the playgue. His temper doth draw thinne and without ado he doth sette forth to London but sayeth it be to barter combe needles but I knoweth that this be false.

The master be awed by the destructs of the grayte fyre which didst stryke London on the second day of

September and doth rayge for 3 fulle days and nyttes. MJ hath moste plezure to see his friend Joseph and his familie doth survive and the fyre didst spare his premises in Wapping and crosseth not the river to Southwark and doth spare his house. The master sayeth that Joseph be muche vexed by attacks on Dutch shippes and must use shippes of Portugal to bringeth wares to London. The master sayeth that the King be stupid and war agin the Dutch wilt be his downfalle.

Even amongst the smoke and ruin neuwe houses be built with bricke and trade doth beginne. MJ doth fynde a haberdasherie shoppe withe needles from Reddich and he doth barter alle and sayeth he wilt barter more if the needles be blunted. Joseth doth see the neuwe combes and desireth to be a partner agayne and wilt paye for 50. MJ doth barter ribbons of many colores and layces for Mary and me.

The master be moste pleased that his friends in Wareham mayketh goode profits by such efforts as combes, and rules that be marked so smalle as 100 partes of the inch and a nonius rule that Will doth call a caliper.

Will and Jake hath the fancie to fasten yron or woode together and MJ doth ponder such in the Pharma tille nytte but I calleth him to bed for I needeth his comforts.

On the morrow the master spake to me of a fancie which be beyonde my mynde for tis a neuwe manner of thinkinge. He sheweth to me a broom withe cord arownde the handle and sayeth that Jake doth want the sayme in yron. MJ then sayeth that the devyce to mayketh the piece needeth to be mayde by Jake who doth neede the piece to matketh the devyce. My head be in rings and I doth laffe and then the master asketh what cometh firste the chicken or the egg. That be the matter MJ doth ponder.

Prayse be to the Lord that I hast a simple mynde.

Sunday 21 October 1666

Meanwhile Jane continued to write her memoirs, far removed from the calamities in the big city. Fortunately, the plague hardly touched the west of England generally, only one family in Wareham, and Tyneham escaped completely. The isolation of rural communities has its compensations. Again there is a long unexplained gap between this memoir and the previous one and no mention of Christmas 1665 either.

Jane tells us that the road to Wareham is now complete, and how pleasurable it is to take their new carriage to the town for shopping. The 'carriage' turns out to be a two-seater, two wheeled trap (with springs), drawn by the doctor's horse. She mentions the trip takes less than an hour.

It seems that Mary spends much of her time practicing with the harpsichord and played melodies for the pleasure of the doctor.

Jane has developed a passion for growing flowers and herbs, again because she knows it pleases the doctor.

The doctor was desperate to have news of his friend Joseph Vanderhoek and his family who he had last seen almost two years ago, but he wasn't prepared to risk his life until the plague was completely over. He was worried, and the girls knew it. Eventually his patience ran out and he decided to make a trip to London just to see Joseph, although he used the excuse of needing more needles for the new fine toothed combs that Rutty, William and Jake were making.

The citizens of London had been decimated by the Great Plague and to make matters worse a fire started in Pudding Lane in the city on Sunday 2nd September 1666, after a very long hot, dry summer. The doctor predicted the plague accurately, but it didn't need a genius to predict that fire was an accident waiting to happen. Indeed the authorities knew it would happen and even trained a group of fire fighters and had rudimentary 'fire engines' with water tanks and pumps with hoses. They even had a last resort strategy to destroy property to create fire breaks. Sadly none of these precautions were put into effect because the Mayor of London failed to invoke them soon enough.

The fire raged unchecked until Wednesday 5th September and destroyed practically every building within the city walls. John was overjoyed to discover that Joseph Vanderhoek and his family survived both the plague and the fire. The fire didn't even reach his warehouse in Wapping and didn't cross the Thames to

Southwark, so he was able to resume business as usual, although staff would have been hard to find.

John found a haberdashery shop that sold needles and he purchased their entire stock. He learnt that the needles were made in Redditch, a small town in the Midlands. John told the owner he wanted needles without points and gave the owner the name of Joseph Vanderhoek as a contact to purchase such needles. Joseph had already placed an advance order for a large quantity of the fine toothed combs because he could see a big market in Holland.

Joseph was very upset by the 'war' between England and the Dutch, which was provoked by the King despite the ravages of the plague and the great fire. Fortunately the battles raged at sea rather than on land, with each side claiming significant minor victories. Dutch merchant ships were 'legitimate targets' in times of war, which forced Joseph to use neutral Portuguese ships to transport his cargoes to and from Holland. The doctor dismissed the stupidity of the King and predicted that war with the Dutch would result in his downfall. Once again history proved the doctor's prediction was correct. In 1688 the King was de-throned and replaced by the Dutch King, William of Orange.

John also bought a considerable quantity of coloured ribbons and laces for the girls to decorate their dresses.

Back in Wareham, John had become a celebrity for building the new road and for his actions during the quarantine episode.

John's 'brain storming' team speeded up the comb manufacturing process, probably using wooden clamps and fixtures to hold the needles until they had been soldered in place. The whole team was now working as a collective. Joseph's large order was obviously very well received. They were also making standard wooden and brass rules engraved with scales as fine as one hundredth of an inch. William was also making engraved brass calipers which he called Nonius rules, which was the name used for Vernier scales at the time. Such calipers would have enabled the team to measure thousandths of an inch accurately, and would have commanded a very high price. The team was making good money on top of their normal businesses.

The clock-maker had an idea to make fastening or clamping devices for holding metal pieces together (nuts and bolts), which he calls 'boys and girls' (clearly a man with a sense of humour). He already made tiny ones in brass for clocks, but Jake wanted to make much bigger ones in iron. Jane only mentions this because the doctor spent the evening in his 'pharma' pondering the problem, but she wanted John to know that she missed him while he was away.

In the morning the doctor tried to explain the nature of the problem which Jane probably found hard to put into meaningful words because she barely understood the concepts. He wound a length of cord around a broom handle and told her that this was what he wanted to make but in iron. To do this he needed a special device to cut the spiral in the iron. The real problem was making this spiral cutting device because he needed such a device in order to make one. He asked her which came first, the chicken or the egg? She could see his dilemma but was most amused by his question.

CHAPTER 21
The lathe

Munday 24 June 1667

The master hath much to ponder and didst hyde in the Pharma tille darkness on mennie a day withe mennie paypers and numbers and drawings. There be so mennie that his mynde muste be fulle. Mary and me taketh foode and wyne to the master but oft it be not tuched. Tis a grayte worrie. Mary be wearie of the wayte and doth creepe in the pharma and sit in the lap of the master with her petticotes aloft and doth draw out his seede but she be so loude alle Tyneham canst heare. I wayte in goode grayce and less haste for the comfort of the bedchaymber.

After a weeke the master cometh forth in glee for the matter be done and doth haysten to Wareham to giveth Rutty the parts to mayketh in woode and later the sayme to be caste in yron. Jake hath the taske to mayke the yron smooth and flatte and Will doth confirm the goodness of the werke withe a glasse in his eye to match the numbers of the matter that MJ hath putte to payper. The 3 gentlemen doth werke as one, as if them doth know the mynde of the master.

MJ telleth to me that Rutty doth mayke the parts in woode for a stronge yron box (that) be called a keep sayfe for our jewelles and paypers of value and William wilt maketh the locke.

The master doth sayle to London with the wood parts to be cast in yron and stayeth with Joseph tille they be done. Joseph be beste pleased after the Dutch fleet hath destroyed the English fleete at Chatham in June and the war be over. I know not if this be goode or bad but the master doth foretelle that the King must counteth his days. I doth putte my truste in the master not the King. In London the master doth telleth Joseph of his neuwe roade to Wareham and they talketh muche of a neuwe companie to builde a hye classe roade to Bristol which be so quicke and mayketh muche profit. The master also hath a fancie to build signal towers along this roade to send quicke messages. I knoweth not how this be done, but the master doth know.

Later by some weekes after the master doth return from London he cometh home withe 2 small yron *partes. So little for alle the werke and calleth them boy and girl. I asketh MJ why they be called so and he doth putte the 2 partes together which mayketh Mary to laffe aloude and then I doth see the matter of her merriment for the 2 parts together doth look lyke warminge which mayketh me to laffe. The boy part doth look lyke a thinne sticke with a cord arownde which doth fit tyte insyde the girl part by twistinge.*

I doth see in the eye of the master that the matter be not done yette.

The hevie yron keep sayfe tis hid below stayrs and adjoyned to the wall with boy and girl parts which canst be taken apart from the insyde alone. On the fronte of the keep safe there (be) 4 brass nobbes with numbers arownde. MJ telleth 2 numbers to Mary and 2 numbers to me. If we doth sette the numbers ryte then the door of the keep sayfe wilt open. Insyde there be a woode box made by Rutty with a locke and key to hold matters of value and promiss notes of the goldsmithes and bagges of gold and silver and purses of Mary and me and our jewelles.

Thanks be to the Lord who doth give our master a wonderous mynde.

Munday 24 June 1667

Janes memoirs now seem to be almost an annual event rather than the earlier monthly editions. Perhaps she thought that her mundane life was unimportant or not interesting enough to write about.

Jane doesn't say that the doctor discussed his 'chicken and egg' problem with his team in Wareham, but I think that it is a safe bet that he did. In engineering terms they needed a Besson screw cutting lathe. There is every chance that William knew and possibly had such a lathe because the technology was already a hundred years old. No doubt the Huguenots brought it with them from France, but William's lathe would have been a tiny hand or treadle powered clock-makers lathe.

I think it is another safe bet that John would have done some very detailed drawings of what was required to make such a lathe suitable for working with iron, based on the way he has always reacted to previous problems.

A lathe, in case you don't know, consists of four parts: a firm base to attach the 'posts' to, a post with a rotating centre to which the workpiece can be attached, a post with a sharp point (rotating or fixed) to steady the workpiece, and a post to keep the cutting tool steady.

The flat bed was no problem at all. Rutty could easily make a pattern in wood which could be cast in iron by any foundry. Obviously Jake would have to clean it up and file and polish it flat by hand. William was on hand to check its accuracy.

The steady post with a fixed point was again no problem because they could do the same as the flat bed.

The rotating head was more of a problem, but even here they could have used a brass-on-brass sleeve bearing as a temporary measure. William could certainly make these, because he already made small versions for clocks. The bearing wouldn't last long but long enough to make a steel-on-brass bearing to replace it. The post holding the bearing was no problem, and likewise fixing the workpiece to the bearing could be done in a number of ways.

Finally the tool post could be make from castings based on wooden patterns like all the other posts. We don't know if the first lathe had a screw cutting system on the tool post, but we do know that this was eventually fitted. More than likely the screw cutting attachment was made in wood by 'Rutty' on a pole lathe and cast in iron from that pattern. Again in all probability the iron version would have been finished by hand by Jake or even William before mounting on the tool post. This cast iron version would have been used to cut a proper steel version to replace the cast iron original.

The reason why they would need to cut screw threads is that the cutting tool would need to be firmly attached to the post holding the cutting tool. In order to move the tool post radially or transversely some sort of screw thread would be required. In the case of a wood turning lathe the tool is normally held by the craftsman using the tool post as a rest so no threaded parts are required. Metal turning requires to tool to be held much more firmly. The srew adjustment that controls the transverse movement of the tool can easily be linked to the main drive so that the tool post moves as the work-piece turns. This is the way a screw thread is machined.

I recognise that there are a lot of assumptions here, but we do know that the doctor sailed to London with a number of wooden moulds to have them cast in iron because Jane tells us so. We also know that at least the original lathe was turned by hand with a long pole to make some of the rotating components such as the main bearings.

At the time of the doctor's visit the Dutch fleet sailed up the River Medway and virtually destroyed the English fleet between 9th and 14th June. After this humuliating defeat by Admiral de Ruyter, the English quickly settled for peace. This was effectively the beginning of the end for Charles II. In 1688 he was deposed by William III of Orange, which secured a lasting peace with the Dutch.

During this visit, the doctor discussed with Joseph the success of his new road to Wareham and they talked of starting a company to build a first class paved road to Bristol. On paper, a toll road looked like a profitable business. The doctor also suggested building 'signalling' towers along the route. Jane gives no clues as to how this 'signalling' system would work, but some twenty years later Robert Hooke produced a comprehensive proposal for an optical semaphore system. More than a century later Claude Chappe, a French engineer, perfected such a system that covered France with a network of 556 semaphore towers. A similar system was operated by the Admirality that connected London to Deal, Yarmouth and Portsmouth between 1808 and 1816. An improved version was later built between London and Portsmouth and operated between 1822 and 1847 when it was replaced by an electric telegraph. As usual, the doctor was two centuries ahead of his time.

In the period between October 1666 and June 1667 the team had solved the 'chicken and egg' problem and had built themselves a screw cutting lathe capable of working iron. A giant step in iron working technology, achieved by a series of small simple steps that progressively improved the device that they were building. The steps were simple common sense but the outcome was spectacular. This was a fundamental principle: incremental evolution.

It seems very clear to me that the doctor had the vision to appreaciate that it is all very well inventing things but the idea itself is of no practical use until you make one. His ideas required precision so he knew he had to to build precision tools. I suspect this vision wasn't so obvious to the three craftsmen: they were merely acting under the guidance of the doctor.

The doctor came home one day and very proudly presented Jane and Mary with a bright shining 'boy and girl' each. Jane asked why they were called 'boys and girls' and the doctor slowly put the two parts together. Mary was the first to make the connection and squealed with laughter. Jane eventually got the joke. Jane later refers to them as B's and G's.

Now that the team could manufacture screw threads, it would not have taken the doctor long to apply this idea to the rotating head to grip the work piece firmly, although Jane does not mention this in her account.

The doctor must have also realised that he had opened Pandora's box: they had nothing to drive their new machine except man power.

The first use of the B and G parts was to secure the heavy cast iron strong box (safe), concealed below the stairs, that the doctor had designed and that Rutty made the wooden patterns for. The safe was bolted to the walls of the house with the nuts on the inside of the safe. Whilst the enormous weight of the strong box and the fact that it was bolted to the house walls would have deterred most thieves, there was a fatal flaw in its design. Cast iron is very brittle and a few blows from a sledge hammer would have cracked it open. The doctor was not aware of this flaw and neither would thieves have been.

It appears that William, the clock maker, had made a numerical combination lock for the safe. Mary knew two of the numbers and Jane knew the other two. The girls also kept their valuables and any saved money in the safe. Likewise the doctor kept important papers, bullion promise notes and gold and silver coins in the safe. It is important to remember that this was a cash society: there were no banknotes and no credit cards. It is a measure of the doctor's trust in the girls that he passed on the combination to them.

Once again we see that the doctor is out-of-step with the times in his attitudes towards women. Not only did he treat the girls as social equals, but he also entrusted his wealth to their safe keeping. In effect he and his two girls shared a joint account, more than three centuries before such a concept would be considered normal.

Some might say that the doctor was foolish and too trusting, but I think the doctor knew exactly what he was doing. These were two very pretty but simple country girls who had been brain washed by society of the time to show defference and respect to high class gentry. Moreover, the girls were very well aware that their good fortune and lifestyle was entirlely dependent on the doctor. They knew what poverty was like and would do nothing to jeopardize their present, comfortable situation. The fact that both girls were clearly in love with the doctor merely compounded their devotion and loyalty to him.

CHAPTER 22
The steam piston

Tewsday 14 July 1668

A yeare passeth and the master doth repaire to the pharma some days but betwixte his mynde be werkinge withe a neuwe matter. I asketh MJ the nature of the matter and he sayeth that the neuwe laythe that doth mayke the boy and girl parts be slowe for it be the werke of 2 men and a turninge pole which be lyke a pump handle.

I be just a simple woman but I sayeth by mornings I doth pump the water to the butte in the roofe. Canst not the water in the butte mayketh the pump handle ryse and falle if it doth werke backwards. The master doth admire so grayte my fancie that he doth rayse my petticotes and warmeth me apon the kitchen tayble in the instante.

Mary doth complayne that the master loveth his devyces but such canst not warm as she.

The master telleth me that William hath much knowledge of the laythe and doth give them the fancie to ajoyne a millstone of grayte wayte and a bar with holes at each end which be called a cranke that mayketh a round motyon from the pump handle to the laythe. The master sayeth with muche joy the cranke and millstone impruffe matters beyonde measure. Now at the forge layborers assemble for easie werke at the pump on days of rayne and Rutty hath chaynged his pole laythe to werke the sayme.

At one tyme the master doth tayke us to Wareham to witness a contest twixt 3 goode strong men who pulleth 100 pounds of stones in a sack upwards for 3 feete for 10 tymes. William be asyde with a pendulum to assay the quickest. The winner be payed a silver which be drunk in ale in the taverne. The master sayeth that this be a measure of the werke of one man which twice be the size of the steam pump for the neuwe laythe.

Twas Jake who calleth at the house with a lamp of brass and a neuwe yron pump which hath such a fynne polish that it doth look lyke silver and he be moste prowde. Tis easie to pump and doth be more quicke to fill the butte. Jake doth tell us there be rings of brass insyde to fit better and to chaynge if they be worne awaye.

Jake doth tell of a kettle that he mayketh of yron to putte steam in a pype with a wayte atop which hangeth *from a beam and keepth the kettle sayfe from blastes lyke a cannon, and the steam be put in the pump with a neuwe slydinge devyce .*

Methinkes Jake doth tayke a fancie to Mary and doth chatter with nowte ende. The pump be moste goode but we know nowte of the other devyces.The lamp be in the pharma on the tayble for the master to see better his werkes. Jake asketh us to telle the master that Will hath engrayved the wheel on the laythe that holdeth the work with a scale that be accurayte to 50 parts of a degree but I know not what be the meaninge of this.

Jake sayeth to me that he hath discover a waye to twisteth rods of yron for to bore moste accurayte holes and Rutty doth use the rods in the neuwe lathe to bore large holes in thicke woodes and ajoyne them with dowels that doth fit so tyte.

Prayse be to the Lord for alle goode fancies.

Tewsday 14 July 1668

This memoir was written a year later after the doctor and his team in Wareham built their lathe. Clearly the rural pace of life at the time held little to inspire Jane to write very often. In fact it was probably the contest in Wareham that prompted her to write this memoir.

Turning the lathe by hand with a ratchet lever at a quarter turn each stroke was incredibly arduous and slow, even if he hired labourers to do it. It probably took half a day just to make one B and G. It was self evident that he desperately needed a rotating power source. Unfortunately he lived in a apart of the country devoid of water mills. The doctor obviously knew about wind mills but probably dismissed them because none were within easy reach. He could have shipped his machine to a part of the country that had a suitable head of water or a powerful windmill, but we have no indication that he even entertained this idea. Personally I think that the doctor would have been put off by the thought of transporting iron goods across country in view of the poor roads. He needed a local source of power close to his craftsmen.

Mary complained many times that the doctor spent more time with his devices than he spent with her, although she had no fear of this competition because nobody could warm the doctor better than she. Jane probably felt the same, but at least she tried to help with suggestions. She reasoned that every day she pumped water up to the butts in the roof, so surely it would also work backwards: the water in the butts could make the pump go up and down. It would only have taken the doctor seconds to calculate the impractical height of the butts required to replace two men working the ratchet lever that turned the lathe. Nevertheless she was instantly rewarded for this suggestion by being 'warmed' on the kitchen table.

It was an idea from William to fit a millstone as a flywheel and to attach a crank to the ratchet lever, because he was familiar with these mechanisms, according to Jane's account. Continuous rotary motion made all the difference to the production of Bs and Gs. Labourers formed a daily queue outside the forge in the hope of easy pay 'cranking' the lathe. Rutty even modified his own pole lathe to work the same way.

In a way, Jane probably was responsible for planting the idea of using a pump to power the lathe. We have no clue what inspired the doctor to put steam in the pump instead of water, although he must have known that steam pressure was more convenient than a very high head of water. All we know is that the doctor and his team started to work on a very accurate piston and cylinder.

We know this because the doctor took the girls to market in Wareham along the new road, to see a comtest organised by his team. There was a large crowd gathered around William who had a pendulum mounted on a wooden stand which also had a stout post. On the post was a wooden pulley with a sack of pebbles at one end of a rope and a wooden bar at the other end. The rope was arranged around the pulley so that a man could pull the rope horizontally to lift the sack of pebbles weighing one hundredweight (112 pounds). Jake invited the crowd to see how quickly they could lift the sack three feet in the air ten times without moving their feet. William timed each player with his accurate pendulum. The prize would be a silver shilling. Jake was inundated with eager hands and he picked three of the strongest.

William announced the happy winner who dashed off to the nearest tavern. Sadly, Jane doesn't tell us what his time was so we don't know what the manpower unit was in terms of modern units.

John explained to the girls that they were measuring the rate at which a man could work. Their lathe needed two men to work it so they could now work out how big the steam pump had to be to replace the men. John may have called it a steam pump, but we would know it better as a steam engine.

James Watt is often credited for inventing the steam engine in 1781, more than a century after the doctor. In fact Jeronimo Beaumont patented a steam engine in Spain in 1606, so even the doctor wasn't the first, and not long afterwards Thomas Savery built one in 1698 followed by Thomas Newcomen in 1712. What this really tells us is that the force pump for pumping water had been around for centuries and it was only a matter of time before somebody thought of putting steam into it instead of water. What held the idea back for so long was that metal working technology wasn't good enough to make practical steam engines until Watt did it with his ten horse power engine, and even then it was crude by the standards achieved by the doctor. What the doctor did was to create accurate technology first and then use this to make the engine.

Basically if you can make a nut and bolt then you can make anything. The main reason we don't know about the doctor and his achievement is that he was so advanced that there was no demand for his capabilities. Steam engines were invented to meet the demand from mining and transport. The industry of the doctor's time was rudimentary: it wasn't ready for the technology that the Wareham team had developed. The Industrial Revolution was bound to happen: it just had not happened yet.

Jane's account also mentions that Jake very proudly presented her with a brand new iron force pump for the kitchen which was much smoother, required less effort and filled the butts faster. The fact that the iron pump looked like silver indicates that the craftsmen had already learnt the trick of 'water polishing' turned parts with a very fine cut at high speed.

She also mentions that the steam is fed to the piston by means of a sliding device (slide valve) which suggests the steam pump was double acting. Jake also told her that the pump could be taken apart and the 'rings' could be replaced if they wear.

If we examine this tiny fragment of information we can say that the piston must have fitted the cylinder very accurately, which we would expect from their new lathe, hence a smoother stoke. Less effort would be required if the piston was made of brass and the cylinder of steel. The fact that the butts filled quicker means that the piston fit inside the cylinder was better allowing less water to by-pass the piston, or it could be the bore was slightly larger. The most telling part is the mention of replaceable 'rings'.

Clearly the team had perfected a method of rolling iron sheet into cylinders and welding the seam, followed by very accurate turning and boring on their lathe. They were certainly able to machine a steel piston to at least ten thousandths of an inch to fit the cylinder, but they would have had problems with wear. If they had tried the same with a brass piston they would have run into problems of differential expansion. The use of brass 'rings' on a steel piston solves both of these problems.

The fact that Jake mentioned that they could be replaced suggests that these rings were split rings (much easier and quicker to replace).

We don't have any details of the 'slide device' (except for a tiny sketch) but I assume it was some kind of slide valve or piston valve. There are no other details, which is a pity because the valve gear is crucial to the way a steam engine works.

The fact that the team had taken the trouble to measure 'manpower' demonstrates that the doctor was designing his engine with a specific output rate in mind (the work equivalent of two men).

The team had achieved all this, so they were more than capable of making a steam boiler that could raise a pressure of say 20 psi. They had no pressure gauge so we have no way of knowing what pressure they actually used. We do know that they also had the technology to produce good check valves. Assuming the cylinder was 2 inches bore and had a stoke of 6 inches then this would have generated about 1.25

horse power at 60 strokes per minute. This would have been enough to power their lathe.

William was a clock-maker so they could easily make cast iron gears to increase this speed if necessary. These would have been based on simple wooden patterns made by Rutty. William would have been particularly interested in making thin sheets of brass for building clocks and gears, and since they could now turn and polish steel rollers it is likely that they had a 'mangle' that could roll brass sheets accurately. They could also use these sheets for making rolled brass pipes with soldered seams that could withstand pressures up to 130 psi before the solder melted, as well as 'spinning' thin brass sheets against a wooden form to make the body of an oil lamp.

Jane's account also mentions that William had engraved the rotating clamp that held the work-piece which was in the shape of a wheel. The rim of this wheel was engraved with a scale that was accurate to 50 divisions of a degree. The ability to mark accurate radial measures would have been very important to William as a clock maker, but it is unlikely that the others appreciated the value of this radial scale at the time.

We have no details at all about the boiler that they used to raise steam, other than it was charcoal fuelled and that it had a relief valve: a weight on the end of an open pipe suspended on a cord from a beam in the forge. We know this because Jake fancied Mary and would chatter at length regardless of whether the girls were interested or even listening. This is not surprising because the girls were attractive, healthy, always immaculately dressed in clean pressed clothes every day and they didn't stink because they showered every day and they cleaned their teeth too.

Now that they could produce Bs and Gs, a simple cylinder boiler with bolted flanged ends would have been sufficient. If they were using a working pressure of 20 psi then the boiler would be running at about 125 degrees Celsius, which was well inside the working range of the brass pipes. The leather washers in the pipe couplings would not have lasted very long but they were easy to replace.

Tool wear would have been a serious problem because the tool steel would have only been slightly harder than the iron of the work-piece. Possibly, Jake would have been constantly re-sharpening tools on a grindstone. It doesn't require much imagination to put a grindstone on the end of the lathe to solve that problem.

The lathe and steam piston must have been up and running because Jane tells us that Jake used it to 'spin' the brass body of an oil lamp which the doctor kept in the '*pharma*'.

Now that they were able to make nuts and bolts and other threaded parts, a whole new world opened up for the Wareham craftsmen. Nothing was beyond their capability now. They were in a unique monopoly position so it is most unlikely that they would reveal their secret 'process' to anyone. Obviously they would want to make as much money as possible from their new capability. There was nothing new about the lathe or the steam pump so a Patent would have provided little or no protection. What was new was the accuracy and level of craftsmanship in these two devices.

Secrecy is what protected the glassblowers of Murano and the same applied to the craftsmen of Wareham.

It seems that Jake had devised a way to make very accurate twist drill bits which could be mounted in the lathe. Sadly, Jane does not elaborate on how this was done. The lathe was designed and used primarily for machining metal, but clearly Rutty was using it to drill accurate large holes in thick wooden beams. This would have been a difficult and labourious job by hand but would only take minutes in the lathe. I suspect that Rutty also used the lathe to make tight fitting dowels (tree nails) to fit these bored holes. Mass production was not even on the horizon and yet the Wareham craftsmen were already developing the tools and techniques ready for its arrival two centuries later.

CHAPTER 23
London

Saturday 3 October 1668

The harvest this year abounde with apples and wilde fruttes and cyder that even the moste poor hath foode in the bellie and be of goode cheere. Oft the fishermen of Worbarrow doth sayle the boat of the master and fish be aplentie in Tyneham and Wareham.

In the long hot summer we doth laye on the sand or swimme or salye off shore. Tis the fancie of Mary to mayketh modeste shifts in linen for the beach but I be in dismay when the linen be wette for it becometh lyke glasse and hydeth nowte from the eyes of strayngers. The sun doth colore our skinne gold and browne which bringeth much flatterie from alle fowlke.

In the month of July the master tayketh us to London to witness the neuwe buildinge of bricke houses and what be left of the fyre. That citie be moste lowde and fulle with bustle I ever didst see with draynes cutte in alle streets and nowte a corner without more houses on the builde.

The master doth barter a boy and cart to carrie our wares and a purse of silvers to barter. This be to our moste delytte and the cart be filled soon which doth concern the ferryman at the crossinge to the house of Joseph who be forayn and moste polyte even as we be servants.

Mary and me playeth gaymes withe the children of the factor amidst much glee whylst the master telleth Joseph in what manner to joyne the Delft bowle lyke unto the privie at Tyneham. MJ doth tell of the neuwe laythe at Wareham which canst mayke pypes and brasses in grayte ease for the factor.

Mary be moste displeased with our bedchaymber of the nytte that be so far from the room of the master. On the morrow we doth tayke abord alle our barters and sette sayle for home in goode cheere with foodes aplentie whylst we be at anker in the dark hours. I be wearie and sleepeth whyle Mary doth hold her frilles aloft and doth warm in lap of the master even with Robert at the helm which I discover when I doth awayke. The Jezabel sayeth that the wayves giveth straynge goode feelings to her warminge.

I oft ponder why I be not with chylde for I doth warme aplentie with much vigore. I be frit lest I be barren. I asketh of the master to sette the mysterie and he sayeth that I be without infirms and there be mennie matters to be in order afore a chylde be in my bodie. I must wayte and alle wilt cometh in tyme. Mary sayeth that she be in delyte that she hath no chylde for it be a grayte danger and mennie women doth die in the birth and she wilt suuffer without the plezure of warminge. Prayse the Lord for the bountie of the harvest.

Saturday 3 October 1668

Jane tells us that it was another hot dry summer with many visits to the beach and many trips out to sea for swimming. Apples were plentiful and the farmers had gathered another good harvest. When they were not using the boat, Robert and some other fishermen used it for fishing, so fish was also plentiful.

Mary tried to create modest swimming dresses so that they could swim and laze on the beach without a care for who was watching, but linen becomes semi transparent when wet and made nonsense of her idea. Mary had little patience and gave up.

The girls acquired a tan like the previous year and received many flattering comments form villagers and folk in Wareham. The girls were now 24 years old and yet there is no mention of celebrating birthdays. Perhaps birthdays are a modern celebration.

In those days, religion was a much greater part of people's lives than nowadays: in her memoirs Jane always finishes with a short prayer. There was little else to do. The 'church' was the major source of moral, spiritual and even social guidance. The 'church' was intent on stability and keeping the lid on the population, and basically maintaining the *status quo*. Even two centuries later the Church was still keeping the lid on, as the third verse of the well known hymn 'All things bright and beautiful' so clearly illustrates:

The rich man in his castle,
The poor man at the gate,
God made them high and lowly,
And ordered their estate.

Apart from gossip, the 'church' was the primary source of news and government legislation because few people could read or write except the clergy who were in a position of priviledge because they spoke the language of God (Latin). Although the population were basically Christian, they were divided between Catholics and Protestants (Church of England, headed by the King). Despite a bloody civil war between the two factions only a few years previously, in which the State Church triumphed under Oliver Cromwell, there was still residual animosity. As far as we know the two girls only went to church once a week on a Sunday, which they were obliged to do by their contract.

The upper classes had more time on their hands to think of spiritual matters whereas the vast majority worried little about the 'afterlife'. For them life was so miserable and hard that they couldn't get to the 'afterlife' soon enough. Accidents, harsh living, starvation and punishment by the Law of the Land saw to it that thousands experienced the 'afterlife' too soon anyway.

The general population were also deeply superstitious and were constantly looking for signs and omens that might affect their lives. There was also a wide belief in magic and witchcraft. Again we see no sign of this in

Jane's accounts, probably because the doctor considered such beliefs as nonsense. On balance I would suggest that the teachings of the doctor were far more beneficial to the enlightenment of the girls than anything the church or superstition had to offer.

In late July in very calm weather, John and Robert took the girls to London as a treat. The city was more noisy and bustling than John remembered. In fact the whole city was a mad building site, with brick buildings going up at every turn and sewers and drains were being cut to clean up the streets. The streets were packed and shops were trading as never before.

The girls were in heaven and even hired a cart to hold all the boxes and baskets they purchased. The ferryman barely had room enough on his boat as they crossed the Thames to the house of Joseph Vanderhoek. Joseph was as delighted as his children to see John again, and was most polite and courteous to the girls. Jane makes a point that even though the girls were technically servants, Joseph treated them as guests. He invited them all to stay the night, and while he and John talked business, the girls played with his children.

It did not occur to Jane that because the doctor was classed as 'gentry', the girls as his companions, would also be classed as gentlewomen. After all, they dressed the part and looked the part and wore expensive jewelery. Their accents and poor education would have given them away, but my guess is that they said very little and depended on people making the assumption that because the doctor was obviously foreign, that his companions were foreign too. They could get away with standing around looking elegant and dazzling, and just smile from time to time.

Joseph wanted to know how to install the privy basin that John had given him some years earlier. John drew a picture of how the pipes must be fitted and promised to supply the brass pipes and couplings and a force pump, now that he could make them so easily.

Mary was not pleased that she and Jane had to sleep in the same room and not with the doctor, so on the way back home on the boat she waited until Jane dozed off and promptly raised her skirts and sat in the doctor's lap. Jane woke up while they were warming and pretended not to notice. Mary commented that the waves make an usual but pleasurable feeling.

At the end of this account Jane tells us that she is surprised she is not pregnant considering the frequency of her bed warming. She is concerned that she may be barren, so she asked the doctor for his opinion. He replied that she was still having 'bloody days' regularly which meant that she was not barren. Jane pursued the subject and asked why she was not already pregnant? The doctor replied that her time would come. There were many factors that determined whether a woman fell pregnant. Only when all those factors are favourable will it happen.

As far as we know the girls were not knowingly taking any contraceptive measures, so it is curious that neither were pregnant considering the frequency they engaged in sex. The doctor would have been aware of the 'rhythm method' and he probably knew of a number of herbal contraceptives, such as pennyroyal (mentha pulegium) and wild carrot seeds (dacuus carota). At that time herbs were the basic source of virtually all medications, so the doctor would have been well aware of the poisonous nature of pennyroyal and the similarity of wild carrot to hemlock (a deadly poison). We don't know if he used any of these methods, but he was exceedingly fortunate not to have impregnated the girls over seven years. On the other hand he may have been sterile or had a low sperm count. All we can say with certainty is that he had enormous stamina.

Had either of the girls become pregnant, I suspect that the doctor would have spirited them away to Holland to give birth, and would then have legally adopted the child to protect the reputations of both the mother and the child.

This seems to have placated Jane, although it could be a sign that Jane is loking for more in the relationship such as starting a family. Mary, on the other hand is only too pleased not to be pregnant and wants things to continue that way. In her opinion pregnancy was an unnecessary and dangerous risk that should be avoided. It would also mean the end of bed warming, which she was not prepared to sacrifice.

CHAPTER 24
The privy

Munday 17 May 1669

Before the summer we doth sayle agayne to London but firste to Wareham to bringeth aborde brasses and pypes and a box of fynne tooth combes for Joseph the factor which the master doth barter welle and mayketh a goode (profit) for them at Wareham.

The goodlie factor giveth his clerk to ayde us to shoppe. London be alle hustle and bustle as before but the bildinge werrke be less and not so mad. Mary doth declare that we visite a coffee shoppe but the clerk doth say that it be not a place for ladies of high classe suche as we.. We doth barter oranges, shugar, spyces and other exoticks and then we doth fynde Norfolk stuffes which be wonderous cloths that doth feele so smoothe and soft and we doth barter camlet and bombazine and moste beste Italyan silke damask tille the purse be emptie.

In the whyle the master doth cross the river to attende the privie for Joseph. In soone tyme the pypes to the

227

butte from the pump at the kitchen (and) then in some hours the pype downe to the kitchen and the privie be done but alle withe cold water.

After noone we cometh from the shoppes and the master be in the arms of a servant girl for him to show her the manner of werkinge the pump to fille the butte. Mary be moste displeased.

The wife of Joseph doth have the plezure to open the pype in the kitchen which bringeth glee and delyte to her for tis the firste tyme that she doth see running water in her house. Joseph be moste prowde and pleased and doth offer a giffte of a Hooke scope to the master who be most thankfulle. At dinner Josph doth mayke a toast to his son as he doth call the master withe tears in his eyes I doth weepe with joy, and Mary.

The bedchaymber be the sayme but Mary doth creepe thither in the nytte and cometh hither at dawn. The Jezabel be warming agayne.

On the morrow we doth sayle to Tyneham verie wearie and retyre to the bedchaymber with the master to eat exotick fruttes and wyne and much play with our cloths..

Prayse be to the Lord for alle the fynne gifftes

Munday 17 May 1669

The next memoir begins with another exciting trip on the boat to London again to deliver pipes and equipment for the privy being built by John's friend Joseph.

First the boat went to Wareham to pick up the pipes and the pump and small tools to bayonet slot any cut ends. They also took on board some clocks made by William and several oil lamps made by Rutty and Jake, and of course a large box of fine toothed steel combs. Business is business after all.

By this time the doctor would have received ten cargos of Dalmation powder from which he would have made at least £5000 profit: a huge fortune for the times. He was wealthy by any standards and could afford a house, a boat and two mistresses with ease.

The doctor sold all his wares to Joseph for much more than he expected. Joseph also arranged for his clerk to accompany the girls while they shopped. In the meantime John crossed the river to help the builders with the plumbing. In a matter of hours they had the butt in the roof connected to the force pump outside the kitchen standing by a bucket that was filled at the hand pump. By mid afternoon the down pipe to the kitchen sink was in place and in no time a hole was made in the wall to the privy to flush the Delft toilet bowl.

John was in the process of teaching the servant girl how to use the force pump to fill the butt when the girls arrived back. Mary was not happy to see John with his arms around the servant girl.

They retired to the kitchen where Joseph's wife had the pleasure of turning on the kitchen faucet to her wonderment and glee. Joseph smiled and presented John with a 'Hooke scope' (microscope) which obviously delighted the doctor. Jane noticed that Joseph had tears in his eyes.

Jane notes that the building work in London was still continuing but it was not so frantic. The city was as noisy and bustling as ever. She and Mary wanted to visit a coffee shop, but the clerk advised against it because it was not the place for high class ladies. In a way this was a huge compliment to the girls, as the clerk assumed that they were ladies not servants because they looked and dressed the part. They did purchase oranges and other strange fruit and they bought a sugar loaf and small pots of spices.

The highlight of their visit was Norfolk Stuffs (woven woollen fabrics). They loved the sheen on the hot pressed camlet, and the texture of bombazine and damask, but most of all the irresistible Italian silk damask. The purse was empty when they returned to Joseph's house.

Although the two girls were 'servants' (and mistresses), the doctor treated them both with considerable respect and affection, more so than most married women of the time. Jane writes that Joseph too treated them with equal respect. Mary clearly has a jealous streak in her nature but it is never directed towards Jane.

Sometimes, what people don't say is often as revealing as what they do say. Normally a diary is the place where people reveal their inner thoughts even if they are not prepared to voice them in public. There is never any any indication that Jane and Mary ever have any disagreements. Their childhood friendship has even survived sharing the same lover. Clearly they are sharing the housework and cooking equally otherwise Jane would have mentioned it. Jane only mentions that Mary is flirtatious and a brazen Jezabel, but she also depends on Mary's confidence and frankness because she herself doesn't have that degree of confidence. It is always Mary who raises issues with the doctor and not Jane, such as taking on Edwin to do the hard work tending the animals and the gardening. Mary has obviously taken on board the doctor's philosophy with respect to 'equality', whereas Jane still has the remnants of her inbred subservience and inhibitions.

They had dinner together before setting off the following morning. At dinner Joseph toasted his 'son' (the doctor) and his delightful companions. The sleeping arrangements were as before, but this time Jane noticed that Mary arose in the night and didn't return until dawn.

They returned to Tyneham exhausted and excited and immediately retired to the doctor's bedchamber to eat fruit, drink wine and parade for the doctor's pleasure draped in their new fabrics, with barely a pause for a whole day, save for pumping water.

CHAPTER 25
Tragedy

Sunday 12 December 1669

On the second day of November we doth hope the master be back in Tyneham from London but his boat cometh not and methinks that he doth delaye for a storm doth blowe and he be moste sayfe and fulle with care. On the morrow there be no master stille and we be frit with worrie and doth weepe much for our dear gentleman. For mennie days Mary and me taketh turne about to stand apon the cliffe and seeketh in the seas for synnes of the master or his boat but nowte be seen and we praye by the day.

The wife of Robert Miller doth visit us in lyke distress and she hath chldren and needeth foode. We giveth alle we hast and silvers but tis not the sayme as a man. In a lyke manner we hath much treasure and fynne wares but we hast no man to warm us.

I sendeth a letter to Joseph the factor by waye of a shippe at Swanwich, (which) tayketh marble to London and sayeth that our master be loste at sea. He be alle sadness and greefe and doth open his house to us but we say nay for we hast no desyre left.

Tis now December and Christ Mass cometh soon, but we be brokke women beyond joy of the season for the master stille cometh not. There be no neuwes from any place and we must deeme the master be dead with Robert Miller, and the Lord God rest each soule. Our worlde be done and nowte be worth the livinge for my bodie be wearie. There not be equal of our dear master. We doth weepe and morne by day and nytte and shalt never stoppe. Woe be apon us and our hearts be heavie with greefe.

Today Mary doth telle of her dream that the master be a saynt and doth care for us both. She draweth muche comforte from her dream and I doth hope that it be true as she beleffe with suche firmness that it tayketh awaye alle her payne.

May the goode Lord hath mercie on us alle and keepth the master in goode grayce forever.

Sunday 12 December 1669

Understandably, this is the very last memoir that Jane wrote. The doctor and Robert had gone to London at the end of October while the weather was still mild, to

235

see Joseph on business and were expected back on the second day of November. The boat did not arrive and the girls assumed that perhaps the doctor had been delayed for some reason. A week went by and the girls began to fear the worst, that the men had been lost at sea. It was impossible for the girls to accept this possibility and they took turns on the cliff top looking out to sea for signs of the boat. By the end of November even the girls had to admit that the men were not coming back.

Mrs Miller was in tears when she came to see the girls and they gave her money for food. The girls themselves must have been distraught. Their whole world had suddenly fallen apart. Jane's account is very short and tells us little about her feelings other than she and Mary are broken women, although she reports that Mary drew comfort from a dream that their beloved master was a saint who would look after them both. Clearly Mary was convinced her dream was true because she wanted it to be so, whereas Jane would also like it to be true but is not so convinced. I suspect that with time, Mary's vision would become an accepted fact like all legends.

From this point on the girls just disappear into the pages of history. We don't know if they continued to live in the house or whether it was so full of memories that they sold the house and started their lives again elsewhere. They were still very young, unmarried and relatively wealthy. We just don't know. No bodies or wreckage was found so we don't know what really happened to the men or the boat.

We can of course speculate, using contemporary evidence. We know that 1669 had a very long hot summer extending well into October, which is why the doctor felt confident about making the trip and didn't expect any trouble. He was not to know that on 30th October a violent storm hit the north-east coast of England and caused severe damage to shipping, even boats at harbour, as well as widespread flooding. The storm system covered most of north-west Europe and slowly edged south. By 1st November there was a gale force storm blowing from the north-east driving virtually anything afloat in the North Sea from the Baltic to the Scheldt delta at break-neck speed towards the Thames estuary to converge on London. The crews on board these lumbering giants would have been fighting to keep their ships afloat and under control. To make matters worse the estuary is shallow which would have increased the height of the waves.

When the doctor and Robert Miller left at dawn on 1st November they were thirty miles inland up the river Thames and would not be aware of the storm, nor of the damage caused in the north-east. All they knew was that ahead was a hard tacking course almost head on into the wind, but once clear of the estuary the wind would be behind them all the way home. The doctor was very safety conscious so the sails would be reefed to half rig as they set off up the Thames.

As you can imagine, when the cold wind from the north-east met the warm waters of the long hot summer a sea mist was likely, and with little light at dawn, and with a high sea running, and at half rig the tiny boat would have been almost invisible to other ships. In fact the converse is also true because the doctor's boat was very low in the water and in the deep troughs he would be unable to see other ships and on the crests the gale winds would have reduced the visibility even without a mist.

In all likelihood the doctor would not have been overly concerned because his boat was under perfect control and the sails were set correctly for the conditions, the craft was stable and virtually unsinkable. Once beyond the estuary he had a clear run all the way home. What could possibly go wrong?

Whist his craft was completely under control, the same cannot be said for the other ships in the vicinity. Under gale force winds the helmsman of a square rigged merchantman was barely able to steer it. Moreover they were almost certainly overloaded with cargo which would make matters worse and in a sea mist nobody on board would have any idea where they were.

As an example, a few years later in 1688 the Dutch King and future King of England, William of Orange, set sail from Holland with a fleet of 60 ships and in similar conditions, a sea mist and a strong north easterly wind but not a gale, the fleet completely missed their target in Torbay and very nearly missed England altogether before they realized that they were off the coast of Plymouth and heading for the open Atlantic. Can you imagine what would happen if the President, on a Navy ship, was on a mission to meet the Cubans in Havana and completely missed the island and ended up in Barbados?

With so many ships, virtually out of control, converging on the estuary and one tiny boat going the other way, a collision was almost inevitable. A glancing collision with any other ship going in the same direction would only have involved minor damage so the captains of the big ships would not have been concerned about collisions: they had much more immediate problems to worry about. The huge heavily laden merchant ships would not have even heard or felt the impact when the tiny boat was hit and crushed. Any debris on the surface, including the pumice from the hulls would be swept before the storm, down the Channel and out into the Atlantic. Any shouts from survivors would have been drowned by the gale winds. In fact the storm didn't blow itself out immediately, instead we know that it returned on the 5th November and again on 9th November. In these circumstances there was little chance that wreckage would be blown ashore anywhere on the English coast. The New World had a better chance of finding wreckage.

A very sad ending to a genius before his time who died at the age of 32. A gentle, kind and generous man. An intensely loyal man who rose above the social views of his time. A man whose love and friendship touched all who met him. A man of vision, who created technology centuries before its time. His life and achievements raise countless questions that will remain unanswered forever. He came from nowhere and disappeared without trace. An enigma to the end.

Aftermath

Rather than a window on the life and times in the mid seventeenth century, Jane Horton's memoirs are a window on the life of the extraordinary Dr John Leiden. In view of the unusual circumstances surrounding the way the manuscipts came to light in 2015 we have to ask ourselves, are they genuine or are they an extremely elaborate and motiveless hoax?

The basic problem with assessing whether these manuscripts are genuine is that there is no corroborating evidence. As far as I can determine there is no material evidence to support the existence of any of the characters who are named in the manuscripts except for William Petty and Robert Hooke. That does not mean they didn't exist: it just means we don't have any surving records of their existence.

I would have expected the memoirs to contain more details related to the medical activities of the doctor. After all, he did study at the best medical university in the world at that time. It appears that the doctor was more interested in mechanical machines rather than human machines, which I suppose is a reflection of the 'rounded' education he received in Leiden, although he did make an accurate assumption about the transmission of the plague. He could have had many patients in his 'pharma' but Jane didn't write about them other than the incident with the broken leg. The girls and the doctor seemed to have virtually escaped all illnesses and ailments, although to be fair I don't think many people would write about the odd headache or common cold. I certainly wouldn't.

Subsequent historical development has eliminated any trace of the buildings mentioned in the manuscripts, and as far as I know the artifacts produced by the craftsmen no longer exist. This again is not surprising. Wareham was too rural for the expensive products that the clock-maker was producing so he almost certainly went back to London. The carpenter and blacksmith were born and bred locals so they probably stayed in Wareham, but without the drive and motivation of Dr Leiden they probably reverted to their old trades. Dr Leiden was not only the brains of the quartet but also the salesman. Even though they had a unique steam powered lathe, they had no market for what it could make other than the ideas that Dr Leiden came up with. Moreover they didn't have any transport for their goods to their major market (London 300 miles away) other than the catamaran which disappeared with the doctor. This conjecture largely reflects Jane's pessimism for the futrure.

However, in a matter of weeks Mary had resolved the issue of a life of eternal mourning which Jane seems resigned to. In Mary's more optimistic view of the future, The doctor has acquired sainthood and is elevated to the task of guardian angel, leaving the girls to face the world with the balance and odds in their favour.

What we know about Mary is that she is confident, beautiful, charming, defiant and full of brazen cheek. She has an abundance of charisma and could become the star saleswoman of the group even with zero technical ability. Jane on the other hand clearly has organizational and managerial skills with her feet firmly on the ground: she has effectively been running the

Leiden household for the past seven years. Provided the three craftsmen and the two girls mutually recognized their respective strengths, then the girls could have successfully carried on the business. The girls had plenty of money to finance the constrction of a replacement catamarran at Mr Salters yard in Swanwich (he probably still had copies or the original drawings of the lost boat) and this would resolve the transport issue. The girls also had an eternal revenue from Dalmatian insecticide powder and invaluable business contacts through their friendship with Joseph Vanderhoek. It could have worked very successfully.

The three craftsmen were probably gifted with more practical skills than the doctor himself, but what they lacked was the doctor's huge fund of disconnected knowledge from which the doctor was so often able to select and piece together fragments into a cohesive concept. Nothing that the doctor achieved was entirely original, but usually a fusion of existing ideas and technology to produce something that had never been done before. Despite this lack, the group already had enough products to keep them in profitable business for the rest of their lives. History tells us that it took about 200 years before somebody thought of putting a steam engine on a ship so that it was no longer dependent on a favourable wind. Clearly the Wareham craftsmen didn't make this connection.

The steam engine, or the boiler or the lathe or all three could have broken down at any time. It is my assessment that neither Jake nor 'Rutty' had the knowledge or confidence to fix it without the guidance of the doctor. I suspect that for a time they were able to make some large diameter nuts and bolts, but not in large quantities, and in all probability a breakdown ocuured and these wonderful devices just rusted away quietly over the years until finally, 200 years later, the industrial revolution caught up.

On balance I think that Jane's pessemistic outcome prevailed against the optimistic version, probably because despite Mary's talents she lacked one important ingredient; focus. Mary didn't have the almost obsessive dedication, patience and focus of the doctor.

Now let us consider the other side of the coin, that the manuscripts are a hoax. If this is so, then the sheer magnitude of the manuscripts make it an extremely elaborate hoax. Who would gain from the hoax? There is nothing in the manuscripts that would cause us the re-think history: it merely confirms what we already know. Historically it doesn't matter whether the manuscripts are genuine or not. Unlike the Piltdown Man hoax in the early 20th century which perverted our understanding of early human development for 40 years, the Tyneham manuscripts have no such evil intent. Even our view of the development of the steam engine remains intact, simply because the Wareham engine wasn't the first, merely one of several before James Watt eventually developed a commercially viable version. If the manuscripts are a hoax then they can be considered as harmless, romantic historical fiction. This still leaves us with the awkward nagging question; why?

In writing this book, I make no judgements whether the manuscripts are genuine: that is a matter for others better qualified to assess. I have just transcrbed the manuscripts at face value and based my comments on what the manuscripts say. Personally I would be more convinced if the manuscripts were radio carbon dated to the mid seventeenth century.

The sketch

The manuscipts contain 3 unused pages and on one extra page there is a small sketch or doodle in the bottom right hand corner with some annotations written in Dutch. It is my opinion that this sketch was made by Dr John Leiden during the time he was designing his steam pump. In all probability he was making calculations and sketches and over-ran the bottom of the page onto the next sheet below. Probably Jane did not notice the sketch and picked it up with the other blank sheets.

Although engineering drawing conventions had not been established at that time, the doctor would have been able to visualise section drawings. Certainly Jake and Rutty were able to visualise 2D profiles as 3D objects because they worked with lathes, and would therefore understand these sketches of the steam pump. I believe that they show how the sliding piston valves worked on the steam and exhaust sides. I am not an expert in steam engine technology so I cannot say that the valves were unusual or unique. The design is in keeping with the overall philosophy of the doctor:

to avoid fine tolerances unless absolutely necessary. The valves are a departure from the doctor's earlier comments about internal valves. Perhaps he thought that they were not fragile parts with only a fraction of the wear of the main pistion so it would be acceptable to use internal valves.

The valves themselves are very similar to the piston valves in brass band musical instruments such as the cornet and trumpet. Instead of operating the valves with the fingers, they are operated by the steam pump piston itself. The valves are mounted in pairs on the main piston and are actuated by contact with the cylinder heads. The only part that requires accurate machining is obviously the fit of the main pistion within the cylinder.

In the diagram the steam inlet valves are shown at the bottom with a single steam inlet to the chamber between the ends of the main piston. The exhaust valves are at the top and vent through a single stub tube that slides inside the hollow end of the main shaft. All the valves including the exhaust tube are a sliding fit.

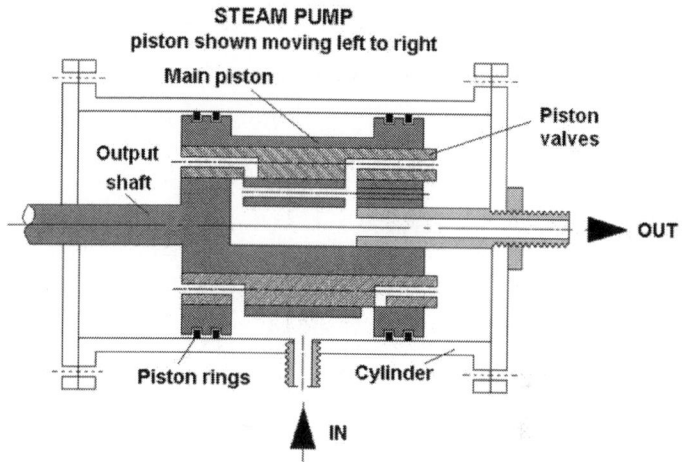

STEAM PUMP
piston shown moving left to right

Main piston

Piston valves

Output shaft

OUT

Piston rings

Cylinder

IN

The arrival of the main piston at the left end causes the left steam valve to open and the exhaust valve on the left to close. The steam valve on the right is closed and the exhaust valve on the right is open. As a result the steam pressure in the left chamber causes the main piston to move to the right with the right chamber vented to atmosphere through the hollow shaft. The diagram shows a plugged channel between the two exhaust valves, but there are other ways to achieve this.

We don't know for sure the actual details of the valve gear, but this sketch just shows which way the doctor's mind was working. The interesting point is that every single component can be made on a lathe or more precisely the Wareham lathe and all the valves are double ended and virtually identical.

There is no indication of any means of speed control probably because there were no pressure gauges at that time. The doctor did have a saftey valve (a weight on an open pipe) which could have been used as a crude pressure gauge by using a succession of smaller weights

There is no mention anywhere about the exhaust steam from the pump, but I think we can assume that the doctor would not have wasted all the heat energy in this steam and would have eventually fitted some form of condenser and re-used the water, and probably would have re-injected this water back into the boiler.

My own view is that since his boat was so important to the doctor, I suspect adding a steam pump to drive it would have been very high on his list of priorities. Toogood and Hayes had already patented a helical screw propeller in 1661 and Robert Hooke also knew about screw propellers, so it is very likely that the doctor also knew. Adding an engine to his boat to make it independent of the wind, would have been an objective very close to the doctor's heart. Sadly he died without passing on this vision to his friends.

Language usage

Jane, the writer of the manuscripts, was a young woman who had no formal education. It is true that she was being tutored but we don't know how well. From her point of view she was trying to come to terms with English spelling, grammar and vocabulary without the aid of printed examples because books in English were scarce or just not available. Books and pamphlets were plentiful in London but outside they were rare except in the personal collections of the landed gentry, and even in her home life the only books that she had access to were written in Latin. Any teacher will tell you that a child learns to read and write by practice and by familiarity with the printed word so that they learn to recognize word shapes, conventional spelling and contextual usage. The more a child reads the more fluent they become.

Jane was in a position where this avenue was not accessible so she was forced to adopt a strategy based on self-observed rules related to phonetics. All of us know that English is hardly phonetic and its rules are riddled with exceptions so Jane was doomed to be less than successful. However, to her credit she was at least very consistent and her spelling gives an insight into the Dorset pronunciation of certain words of her time, such as 'chair' and 'stair'.

For example in Jane's spelling rules: the long (a) as in make, table, and take are all spelt with (ay) as in the long (a) in the month May. Likewise the long (i) as in vile, iron, and time are all spelt as (y). The other use of the letter (y) as in the word ending (ion) as in position, is spelt (yon) because that is what it sounds like. The final rule concerns the use of the word end (y) as in family, many, and kindly. Jane tends to use (ie) possibly to avoid confusion. Another feature is the liberal use of the silent (e) word ending which was very common at that time.

In terms of grammar, she was guided by local usage and in a rural, poorly educated community the local usage would have been less than correct. This is most evident in the very frequent misuse of the verb 'to do' and the verb 'to be' e.g. 'I do go to the supermarket' as opposed to 'I am going to the supermarket'. Even today in the west of England this construction is still used. Similarly, 'I be going to the supermarket' is another example but still used today. Periodically the old pronouns appear such as 'thee and thou', 'mine and thy' but this is rare. Jane would have been aware of their usage from bible readings at church. Although the King James bible was written in scholarly English of the early 17th century it was not a reflection of common, rural language of the times.

If the word usage and frequency is analysed it becomes evident that Jane's vocabulary is extremely limited, although odd uncharacteristic words do occur, which were probably inspired by her employer John Leiden, who was the major source of her material. In this context we have to remember that her employer spoke Latin and Dutch better than he spoke English and that his accent would have determined the way that Jane spelt unusual words. It is possible that the doctor spoke with a Scottish accent but to Jane any accent would have been strange. In Jane's time every town probably had a characteristic accent. Even today some regional accents are almost incomprehensible.

The word 'nowte' appears frequently and is still used in the north of England, meaning 'nothing' or 'very little' and is equivalent to the word 'nought' in the English of today. It is probable that Jane pronounced this word as nought. The word 'frit' also appears in the text, meaning 'frightened' or perhaps 'apprehensive'. Again it is a word that is still used in parts of England today. The word 'quaint' is an Elizabethan relic meaning beautiful and fell from general English usage by the end of the 17th century although real estate agents (realty agents) often describe ancient cottages as 'quaint'.

Understandably Jane's writing lacks any literary style and is basically a collection of short sentences, because she is writing about events as she recalls them rather than attempting to assemble them into a structure. Probably, as a result of tuition, she later attempts a more flowing style by compounding sentences but this merely makes the text more difficult to read and understand because clauses are often misplaced and unmarked by punctuation.

Lastly we have the curious absence of deletions or corrections. On reflection this may not be so curious after all. Writers only cross out words or make corrections if they know or believe they have made a mistake. How would Jane know that she had made a mistake? She had no books on grammar and dictionaries did not exist. She wrote as she spoke and spelt as she thought words sounded. For her, there was no correct or incorrect way and therefore no need for corrections.

ABOUT THE AUTHOR

J. Randolf Scott, a retired Chemical Engineer, and father of five children, lives in the heart of rural England. A prolific inventor and innovator, the author is also an artist and a Fellow of the Institution of Analysts and Programmers. In his own words, "As an artist I paint what I see, and in my books I paint in words what I see in my mind". During his career he has travelled to most countries in the world, and this is reflected in the scope and subject matter of his writing. His novels cover a wide range of genres, from thrillers, to period romance and science fiction, and he admits that background research often takes much longer than writing the novel itself. This is the first non fiction work by this author who until now has written ten fiction novels in a variety of genres. Normally the author spends a great deal of time researching the background to his novels. In this case he spent even more time researching the historic background to the memoirs in order to write a meaningfull commentary to the manuscripts.

22249917R00149

Printed in Great Britain
by Amazon